Ben Hamilton is one of Britain's top puzzle makers and for years was the Puzzles Editor of the monthly magazine *Games and Puzzles*. His problems and puzzles have appeared in newspapers and magazines on both sides of the Atlantic.

BRAINTEASERS AND MINDBENDERS

BEN HAMILTON

A FIRESIDE BOOK
Published by Simon & Schuster
New York London Toronto Sydney Tokyo Singapore

FIRESIDE

Rockefeller Center
1230 Avenue of the Americas
New York, New York 10020

British edition © 1979 by Victorama Limited
U.S. edition © 1981 by Prentice Hall Press

Published in 1986 by Prentice Hall Press
Previously published by Prentice-Hall, Inc.

First Fireside Edition 1992

Manufactured in the United States of America

30 29 28 27 26 25 24 23 22 21 20 19

Library of Congress Cataloging-in-Publication Data

Hamilton, Ben.
  Brainteasers and mindbenders.

  1. Puzzles. 2. Word games. I. Title.
GV1493.H26   793.73   81-1748
AACR2

ISBN: 0-671-76199-4

A puzzle for every day of the year!

Introduction   *ix*

January

1

February

14

March

25

April

37

May
49

June
61

July
73

August
84

September
96

October
108

November

120

December

131

Solutions   *145*

Introduction

The puzzle is one of the best types of game. Not only does it stop you doing something useful, and can actually keep you from your work for whole *hours* at a time, but if you are fortunate enough to "win" and solve the wretched teaser, you don't have to tell anyone about it—so it's almost as good as losing! If, on the other hand, you are naturally competitive, and enjoy a challenge, you can sit quietly in a corner with your puzzle or brainteaser, and all the pressures and tensions of the contest can seethe within as you wrestle with the problem, until that ecstatic moment when you solve it. Then you slump back into your seat with a smile of exhausted but self-satisfied triumph on your face.

For those who don't think that tackling a puzzle matches up to the competitive thrill offered by the experience of running around, with other grown men or women, after balls of various sizes, let me assure you that the puzzle can not only be a most rewarding pastime, but is now actually an "in" thing. In fact, some of the most popular programs on TV are constructed round party games and puzzles. The mass audience show is the Brainteaser!

The time has come to look on puzzles as a social asset, ideal for breaking the ice on long journeys. So my advice is to learn a few by heart. Picture the scene . . . a crowded train compartment, filled with silent commuters tired after a long day. Enter another such commuter, except that he has a spring in his step and a light in his eye. Courteously, he introduces himself, shaking hands with all the passengers. He settles himself down, and immediately senses that the atmosphere needs pepping up. "How many words can we get out of BRAINTEASER?" he says, turning with enthusiasm to his neighbor. "Come on, BAT, RAT, RESTRAIN; oh, there's so many." Soon the air is filled with many cries of "TAR," "SEAT," "ARAB," "RABIES," BEARSKIN," "You can't have that, there isn't a K," "BERATE," and so on. "Are you allowed proper names?" and so on. The tedious journey has gone in a flash.

My dictionary defines a puzzle as "a puzzling question," which doesn't help much, but goes on to add that it is "contrived for the purpose of exercizing ones ingenuity and patience." What is a little more surprising is that apparently a puzzle is also—and I quote—"a piece of wood, about a foot long, fastened to the lower jaw of a dog or horse, so that the pointed end projects in front, and prevents him from putting his head close to the ground."

Finally let me leave you with the example by Ivan Morris, no mean puzzler himself, of the man from Mars who says to his friend, "As if that lot didn't have enough unsolved problems already, they have to go and invent useless ones about blind Japanese professors in mazes, and men being each other's uncles . . . " Maybe some of the problems on earth are insoluble, but the ones that follow here are not. So, if you want to escape from your own problems for a while, pick up this book. You can solve some of these problems and then the real ones may not seem half so bad!

Nicholas Parsons

BRAINTEASERS AND MINDBENDERS

January 1

New Year's Day

Below are clues for ten words. Against each clue is an indication of the word's length, and also where the letters JAN occur in the word. See if you can work out what the complete words are. As an example, if the clue was 'a spear for throwing' and the letter pattern was JA — — — — N, you should be able to work out that the answer is JAVELIN.

JAN — — — —	a doorkeeper
JA — — — N —	a shrub with very fragrant flowers
JA — — — N	professional terminology
J — — — — AN —	rejoicing
— — — JAN	a hard-working person
JA — — N — —	a variety of topaz, garnet or quartz
J — — — — — AN	characteristic of the period of James I
— — — JAN — — — —	an imaginary figure of great power
— — J — — AN —	a commanding officer's assistant
— — — J — — A — — — N	union

January 2

Following are some simple addition problems in disguise. Can you substitute a digit for each letter? All identical letters must have the same digit, and all different letters must be replaced by different digits. All of the problems can be worked out logically. (N.B. The four groups of letters are not related.)

```
a.    Y        b. MA
      Y          +A
     +Y          ───
     ──          AM
     MY
```

1

```
c. ON      d.  XXX
   ON        +   B
   ON          ────
  +ON          BAAA
  ───
   GO
```

January 3

Below are the names of ten famous film stars, though the letters of each name have been rearranged. Can you take each of the re-arranged names and untangle it, so as to arrive back at the stars' real names? As an example, if DERBERT ORFORD was in the list, you ought to be able to discover that that was just ROBERT REDFORD in disguise. Just one point: a male name in this list doesn't necessarily imply that you need to find a male film star. And the same goes for female names and female film stars.

Johnny Awe   Fred Peaton
Bryan Tweater   Gerri Gregson
Neal W. Upman   Wildcat O'Stone
Alb Grackle   Thornton Cleash
Eoan Strawer   Bunny Ryler

January 4

Each of the items shown here represents a familiar word, name, phrase or saying. For example, CCCCCCC should be recognized as The Seven Seas. See if you can work out the half dozen here.

a. ADO ADO ADO   b. WORLAMEN
   ADO O ADO
   ADO ADO ADO

c. E
   M
   A
   R
   F

d. ONALLE

e. ONE ANOTHER
   ONE ANOTHER
   ONE ANOTHER
   ONE ANOTHER
   ONE ANOTHER
   ONE ANOTHER

f. ME
   AL

January 5

On one of the escalators in a department store, I find that if I walk down 26 steps, I need 30 seconds to get to the bottom; but if I make 34 steps, then I only need 18 seconds to reach the bottom. What is the height of the stairway in steps? The time is measured from the instant that the top step begins to descend to the time I step off the last step at the bottom on to the level platform.

January 6

In today's jet-age world, we don't have the time for the flowery phrases in which our ancestors cloaked their thoughts. On the other hand, there's no excuse for the sloppy jargon which has become the lingua franca of so much of today's speech. The age of eloquence has given way to the age of insatiable banalities, and we are all the poorer for it. For example, Elizabeth Barrett Browning's "I love thee to the depth and breadth and height my soul can reach" has degenerated to the modern-day "You turn me on!" Can you translate the following quotations from yesteryear into their modern-day equivalents?

"The word must be spoken that bids you depart
Though the effort to speak it should shatter my heart."

3

"God's in His heaven
 All's right with the world."

"Great is life . . . . and real and mystical."

"Joy was swept over my eyes . . . . a fiery broom sweeping
 out of the skies like a star."

January 7

There are 52 distinct patterns which can be displayed by five-letter words. For example, POKER, with no repeated letters, has the pattern 12345; TRUTH, having the first and fourth letters the same, has the pattern 12314; CYNIC, having the first and fifth letters the same, has the pattern 12341; and MADAM, having the first and fifth letters the same, as well as the second and fourth, has the pattern 12321. Now see if you can find examples for the following patterns.

12344	12213	12323	12131
11232	12231	12331	12311
12123	12233	12332	12232
12132	12312	11231	12322
12133	12313	12113	12112

January 8

The taxi driver had been somewhat impolite to his passenger, so the passenger asked for the driver's number, with a view to reporting him.

"So you want my number, do you?" said the driver. "Well, you can work it out for yourself. If you divide my number by 2, 3, 4, 5 or 6, you'll find there's always a remainder of 1. But if you divide it by 11, there's no remainder. What's more, there's no other driver with a lower number who can say the same."

Just what was the taxi driver's number?

January 9

Behead an animal (FOX) and leave an animal (OX).

Behead a musical instrument and leave a musical instrument.

Behead a margin and leave a margin.

Behead a vessel and leave a vessel.

Behead to liquefy and leave to liquefy.

Behead to ascend and leave to ascend.

Behead to move slowly and leave to move slowly.

Behead a woman's name and leave a woman's name; and behead again to leave a man's name.

Curtail a lamentation and leave to lament.

Curtail a protection and leave a protection.

Curtail to blemish and leave to blemish.

Curtail to conceal and leave concealed.

Curtail to disclose and leave to disclose.

January 10

A philanthropist set aside a certain sum of money for equal distribution each week to the needy individuals that he knew. One day he remarked, "If there are five less applicants next week, you will each receive $2 more." Unfortunately, though, instead of there being fewer applicants, there were actually four more persons applying for the gift. "This means," he pointed out, "that you will each receive $1 less."

How much did each of the applicants receive at that last distribution?

January 11

Five smart newsboys got together and formed a partnership, and they disposed of their newspapers in the following manner. Terry

Saunders sold one paper more than one-quarter of the whole lot, Ben Jackson disposed of one paper more than one-quarter of the remainder, Norman Saunders sold one paper more than a quarter of what was left, and Colin Jackson disposed of one paper more than a quarter of what was left. At this stage, the Saunders brothers had together sold 100 papers more than the Jackson boys had sold. Joey Jackson, the youngest of the five boys, now sold all the papers that were left.

The three Jackson boys sold more papers than the two Saunders boys, but how many more?

January 12

In the following sum, replace the letters by digits. One letter always represents the same digit, and no digit is represented by more than one letter. As it stands, there is more than one valid solution, so let us add that WHEN is W raised to the Nth power.

$$
\begin{array}{r}
\text{EAST} \\
\text{WEST} \\
\text{SOUTH} \\
+\text{NORTH} \\
\hline
\text{EARTH}
\end{array}
$$

January 13

When three ordinary words are "telescoped" together, like those given here, it isn't always easy to recognize them, even though their letters are in the correct order. For example, given MINISTETSONS, would you be able to work out that it was made up from IONS, MINT and SETS? Now try the ten given here, bearing in mind that each is made up from three four-letter words.

SCARLETRINGS   FORTYBEAMERS

MAROONTRAMPS   STABLEHEATER
FORTYSLAKERS   OXYGONNESTLY
GREENPILATES   FORTYPLEASES
SPARROWINGLY

January 14

A word or name that is spelled backwards the same as it is forwards is a linguistic curiosity called a "palindrome." Words such as BIB, SEES and MADAM are examples of ordinary palindromes. Many everyday words happen to be palindromes. Listed below are the definitions of 10 such words, with the numbers of letters in each palindrome shown in brackets after the definition. How many of these commonplace palindromes do you recognize from their definitions?

a. a notable achievement (4)
b. not sloping (5)
c. more blood-colored (6)
d. 12 hours after midnight (4)
e. males and females (5)
f. one who resuscitates another (7)
g. narratives of heroic deeds (5)
h. pertaining to public affairs (5)
i. made wet with dew (5)
j. a mechanical part that causes rotation (7)

January 15

Each set of asterisks represents a word made up from the same four letters but arranged in a different order. Can you work out what the six words are?

A****young lady on****bent,
Lowered her****with sly intent.
'****,'she said, 'It's time to play.
What shall we do to****today?'
'My dear,' said he, 'Do as you please.
I'm going to eat St****cheese!'

January 16

Said the teacher to young Johnny, "If a certain missile will hit its target one out of four times, and four such missiles are fired at one target, then what is the probability that the target will be hit?"

"That's simple," answered Johnny. "It's a certainty that one missile will land on target."

What do you, dear reader, have to say about that?

January 17

Did you know that certain pairs of two-digit numbers can have the same product when both numbers are reversed? For example:

$$12 \times 42 = 21 \times 24$$
$$12 \times 63 = 21 \times 36$$
$$12 \times 84 = 21 \times 48$$
$$23 \times 96 = 32 \times 69$$
$$24 \times 63 = 42 \times 36$$
$$24 \times 84 = 42 \times 48$$
$$26 \times 93 = 62 \times 39$$
$$46 \times 96 = 64 \times 69$$

There are six other sets of numbers of this nature. How many of them can you find?

January 18

I am a word of ten letters.
My 1, 2, 8 is rainy.
My 1, 5, 6, 7 is part of a bird's body.
My 8, 9, 10 is a weight.
My 1, 2, 3, 4 is a spring.
My 7, 5, 4, 8 is a golden surface.
My 10, 9, 8, 2 is a short letter.
My whole is a celebrated warrior.
Who or what am I?

January 19

The letters EEFGHINNORSTUVWXZ form the smallest list which can be used, in turn, to spell out the names of the digits ZERO, ONE, TWO, and so on, up to NINE. Notice that two E's are necessary to handle THREE and SEVEN, and two N's are needed for NINE.

Using each of the letters in this list, the following five words can be formed:

FEZ   GIN   RUNT   SHOW   VEX

Can you use the same letters, all of them, to make just four words? Now can you use the letters to make just three words?

January 20

Below are 25 letters of the alphabet, omitting the Q. Starting at any one of the letters and moving one letter at a time up or down or left or right or diagonally, see how many different words you can spell out.

Words should have at least three letters. No word may use a letter more than once. And no proper names, foreign words, abbreviations and plurals, please. Can you find over two dozen words?

A B C D E

F G H I J

K L M N O

P R S T U

V W X Y Z

January 21

If you've already done January 14's puzzle, you will have found out that a word or name that reads the same backward as forward is called a "palindrome." BIB, SEES and MADAM are examples of ordinary palindromes. Listed below are the definitions of 10 such words, with the number of letters in each palindrome shown in brackets after the definition. How many of these everyday palindromes do you recognize from their definitions?

a. to peer through a crevice (4)

b. to blow a horn in rapid blasts (4)

c. musical compositions for a single voice (5)

d. a belief (5)

e. a crazy person (4)

f. the monarchs of Iran (5)

g. made a god of (7)

h. to allude to (5)

i. a stupid, awkward person (4)

j. an electronic method for finding objects (5)

January 22

Quick as a flash, and without reaching for a calculator or pencil and paper, can you divide 987654321 by 123456789? Your answer should be accurate to six decimal places. Try this little puzzle on your friends, and see how quickly they arrive at the answer.

January 23

The verbs BRING, BUY, CATCH, FIGHT, FREIGHT, SEEK, TEACH and THINK share a common property that no other common verbs in the English language possess. What is it? Think — don't look at the solutions section for at least two minutes!

January 24

There are four and twenty blackbirds on the roof of a house. A hunter shoots one of them with his rifle. How many of the blackbirds are then left on the roof? Can you provide four possible answers, explaining your reasoning in each case?

January 25

LAST, LEST, LIST, LOST, LUST — but not LYST. Can you find another set of six four-letter words where three of the letters are always the same and the fourth letter can be any of the vowels A, E, I, O, U and Y?

January 26

A cyclist rode a mile in three minutes with the wind, and returned in four minutes against the wind. Assuming that he always applies the same force to the pedals, how long would it take him to cycle a mile on a windless day?

January 27

Lewis Carroll's birthday (1832)

Apart from writing *Alice's Adventures in Wonderland* and *Through the Looking Glass*, Lewis Carroll published many mathematical treatises and also devised some of the most thought-provoking logical puzzles. A typical puzzle of Carroll's would be to give the reader two true statements, and then ask that some inference be drawn from these. For example, the reader might be told that "No professors are ignorant" and "All ignorant people are vain." The reader was then expected to infer that "No professors are vain." Given below are three pairs of true statements. What inference can you draw from each of these pairs?

a. No doctors are enthusiastic.
   You are enthusiastic.
b. Dictionaries are useful.
   Useful books are valuable.
c. No misers are unselfish.
   None but misers save bottle tops.

January 28

Lewis Carroll, whose birthday it was yesterday, probably invented the pastime of transforming one word into another by changing one letter at a time without altering the positions of the other letters, and always leaving a word at every stage of the process. Such transformations are called "word ladder." For example, FIND could be transformed into LOSE as follows.

FIND
FINE
LINE
LONE
LOSE

Now, can you convert COLD into WARM? And, a harder one, EVIL into GOOD? (Proper names may be used.)

12

January 29

Each of the letters below corresponds uniquely to a numerical digit. Find the correspondence to make this addition correct.

ALPHABET
+LETTERS
SCRABBLE

January 30

Sam Loyd's birthday (1841)

Sam Loyd was one of the great innovators of puzzles. He invented thousands of the most ingenious and popular puzzles ever originated. The following is one of Loyd's puzzles. It was the time of the great annual picnic, and, of course, hundreds of people wanted to go. To accommodate all the people and all the food and drink needed for the picnic, quite a few wagons had to be pressed into service. In fact, every wagon carried exactly the same number of people. Halfway to the picnic site, ten of the wagons broke down, so it was necessary for each of the remaining wagons to carry one more picnicker. At the end of the picnic, when they started for home, fifteen more wagons were found to be out of commission. So, on the return trip, there were three more people in each wagon than when they had started out early that morning. Perhaps you can tell us just how many picnickers there were. And how many wagons did they begin with?

January 31

In each of the following sentences is hidden the name of a country. For example, in the sentence "His painstaking efforts were much admired," the name of SPAIN is hidden in the first two words. Can you find the five hidden countries?

a. Uncle Wilbur made the most of his stay in Brighton.
b. Nahum, Malachi, Leviticus and Haggai are four of the books in the old Testament.
c. In his collection of stuffed animals, young Peter had wombats, ewes, terns, a moa, a dodo, and an emu.
d. He gave Philip inestimable help with his study of Ibsen, egalitarianism and French wine.
e. That well-known bronco star I cast as the cowboy in my film has refused to play the part.

February 1

Below are clues for ten words. Against each clue is an indication of the word's length, and also where the letters FEB occur in the word. See if you can work out what the complete words are. As an example, if the clue was "faint" and the letter pattern was F−EB−−, you should be able to work out that the answer is FEEBLE.

FEB − − − −	feverish
F − E − B − − − − −	one who roves about looking for booty
− − FE − − B − −	that may be deduced
− − FE − − − B − −	that may be protected
− − FE − − − B − −	not practicable
F − E − − B − − − −	knee-length boots
F − − − E − B − − − −	part of a violin
F − − EB − − − −	one who foments strife
F − − EB − − −	to prognosticate
F − − E − − B − −	part of a ship

February 2

Somewhere in *Finnegans Wake*, James Joyce wrote "Gee each owe tea eye smells fish." What Joyce was really saying was that the letters G, H, O, T and I spell FISH. Can you explain why they do?

February 3

Each of the items shown here represents a familiar word, name, phrase or saying. For example, CCCCCCC should be recognized as The Seven Seas. See if you can work out the ten here.

a. ONCE
   8AM
b. REEF9PM
c. POPPD
d. QuakerfairQuaker
e. TRINTIN
f. & LIGHTNING
   TH
g.   S
   EIGN
h. gbo
i. B
j. C
   S Margaret Thatcher

February 4

Want a wooden overcoat? Buy Honest John Whitworth's health-re-energising sulfo-uranyl-impregnated Comfi-Vest with its unique quasi-xyloid fibres. Obtainable only from the Paradise Vending Company, Leighton Buzzard, Bedfordshire, England, and Ninevah Products, Memphis, Tennessee, USA.

Examine these three sentences carefully. Can you see anything odd or significant about them? You can certainly count on there being something peculiar about them.

February 5

Here are five facts about four delightful girls:

a. Bertha is younger than the dancer, who lives directly west of Jemima.
b. The dancer lives directly north of Miss Pugh, who lives exactly five miles from Hattie, who lives exactly two miles from the singer.
c. The pianist is older than Miss Chandler and Chloe is older than the actress.
d. Hattie is older than Miss Judd, who lives exactly three miles from Jemima, who lives directly south of Miss Benn.
e. The fact that all four girls are delightful has nothing to do with the solution to the following two questions.

How far does Chloe live from Bertha? And which girl is the oldest?

February 6

What is unique about this list of words? Why would there be nothing special about them if they were printed in lower-case type?

BEDECKED	HOOD
CHECKED	HOOKED
CHOICE	ICE
COOKIE	ICEBOX
ECHO	KICKED
HEX	KIDDED

February 7

Charles Dickens' birthday (1812)

Solve the following 15 clues. Each answer should be five letters long. The last letter of each answer is the first letter of the next answer. When you have all the answers, take the middle letter of each word. Together they should spell out the name of a character from one of Dickens' works.

a. proportion
b. colored pigment
c. lament
d. desire
e. courage
f. additional
g. fearful
h. deride

i. board game
j. muddle
k. age
l. underworld
m. Greek letter
n. expert
o. weary

February 8

Five children hit on the idea of getting themselves all weighed on an automatic machine at the total cost of just one penny. Two of them got on the stand at the same time, and one of them changed places with another until all the ten possible pairs had been weighed. The weights in pounds were as follows: 114, 115, 118, 119, 121, 122, 123, 125, 126 and 129. The big brother of one of the children then managed to work out their individual weights from these figures. Can you do the same?

February 9

Can you recognize words without their I's? Given below are a dozen words from which exactly 40 I's have been removed. See if you can work out what the words are by putting back the missing I's. Each of the words has three or four I's.

BKN   LBDNST
DVDNG   LMTNG
LLCT   MNKN
NCLNNG   MNMSNG

MSSSSPP   TMDTY
PHLPPC   VSBLTY

February 10

In the year 1928 there were four dates which, written in a well-known manner, the day multiplied by the month will equal the year. These are 28.1.28, 14.2.28, 7.4.28 and 4.7.28. How many times in this century (1901–2000 inclusive) will this happen? Also, which year in the century gives the largest number of dates complying with these conditions? There is one year that beats all the others.

February 11

Here is a well-known English word. Can you work out what it is?

E10100010001000UNI100ATXN

February 12

The word FACETIOUSLY contains the six vowels, A, E, I, O, U and Y, in their alphabetical order. Can you find another English word that does the same?

February 13

"Between two and three o'clock yesterday," said the major, "I looked at the clock and mistook the minute hand for the hour hand, and vice versa. Consequently, the time appeared to be 55 minutes earlier than it actually was. What was the correct time?"

February 14

St. Valentine's Day

Cervantes wrote that the whole alphabet is required of every good lover, and proceeded to list the qualities he had in mind. For some reason, though, he omitted U and X. "Understanding" would have been a good choice for U; and "xenial," meaning "hospitable," would have done for X. Make your own alphabetical list of the qualities you expect of a lover, and see how often you agree with Cervantes.

February 15

How are the following numbers arranged?

    2   3   6   7   1   9   4   5   8

What are the next four numbers in this sequence?

   12   1   1   1   2   1   3   ......

Arrange eight 8's so that when added up they will equal 1000.

February 16

As we saw on January 14 and January 21, a word that reads the same backwards as it does forwards is called a palindrome. If, on the other hand, reading a word backwards produces a different word, we have what is known as a "reversal." Thus, the word pairs GUM-MUG, RATS-STAR and DEVIL-LIVED are examples of reversals. There are many pairs of reversals in English, and you are now about to meet some of them. Following are six pairs of definitions, each pair corresponding to a pair of reversals. Given in brackets after the definitions are the numbers of letters in the words sought. Can you find all the reversals?

Knives, forks and****** (6)
Pries in a sneaking manner (6)

Committed an offense (6)
******the Menace (6)

Rigged, sailing vessels (6)
Small cylinders on which thread is wound (6)

One who refuses to grant something (6)
Checked a horse (6)

Fills with resolution (6)
Partly frozen forms of rain (6)

Diversions or pastimes (6)
Leather bands for sharpening razors (6)

February 17

The numbers 1 to 9 can be arranged in the form of a square, as shown below, so that each row of numbers has a common total, each column of numbers has the same common total, and the numbers in the two diagonals have the same total. This is what is called a "magic square."

```
8 1 6
3 5 7
4 9 2
```

All rows, columns and diagonals in this square add up to 15. Now, can you arrange the numbers 1 to 16 so as to form a magic square? This square will have four numbers in each row, column and diagonal.

February 18

Lovers of poetry with mystical overtones may recognize this stanza:

Wake! For the Sun beyond yon Eastern height
Has chased the Session of the Stars from Night;
And, to the field of Heav'n ascending, strikes
The Sultan's Turret with a Shaft of Light.

It is the opening quatrain of the *Rubaiyat of Omar Khayyam*, as translated by Edward Fitzgerald. What is the essence, substance, or distinctive quality of this passage? What must strike every reader of these lines?

February 19

Here is a word square composed of five five-letter words. Notice that the across words are the same as the down words.

```
C H E S T
H A S T E
E S H E R
S T E E R
T E R R Y
```

Try solving the five clues given below. The answers are all five letters long, and if you take the words in order, you should end up with another word square.

a. Elector
b. It ranges in color from pale yellow to orange and red
c. At that place
d. Went astray
e. Stalk-like

February 20

Certain words can be turned into apt descriptions of themselves by a skillful rearrangement of the letters comprising the word. For instance, ENDEARMENTS is a word that applies most fittingly to TENDER NAMES; VILLAINOUSNESS is obviously the word answering the definition AN EVIL SOUL'S SIN: and a good example of INCOMPREHENSIBLES is provided by PROBLEMS IN CHINESE. Such apposite letter rearrangements are known as "anagrams." Given below are 6 anagrams. Your task is to reconstruct the six original words which were scrambled to produce these anagrams. Remember that in each case, you are required to turn the given phrase into just one appropriate word.

a. Voices rant on
b. A rope ends it
c. Often sheds tears
d. Apt is the cure!
e. Nine thumps
f. Is not solaced

February 21

Though small I am, yet, when entire,
I've force to set the world on fire.
Take off a letter, and 'tis clear
My paunch will hold a herd of deer:
Dismiss another, and you'll find
I once contained all humankind.

February 22

This puzzle consists of pairs of words that are quite different in meaning but are frequently confused with one another. For example, LUXURIANT and LUXURIOUS, and PERSPICACIOUS and PERSPICUOUS. How many of the ten pairs will you be able to recognize?

a. a hospital for the treatment of chronic diseases
   an institution for the promotion of health

b. to reveal
   to depreciate

c. beggary
   dishonesty
d. to command solemnly
   to renounce
e. to irritate or scrape
   to censure or reprimand
f. to rout
   to make uneasy
g. corrupt
   pardonable
h. to write or compose
   to charge with a crime
i. self-pleased
   pleasing to others
j. occurring every two years
   occurring twice a year

February 23

In this little piece of addition, every digit from 0 to 9 is uniquely
represented by a letter of the alphabet. It may be assumed that T
is not zero. Can you work out the values of the various letters?

```
  T W E N T Y
  T W E N T Y
+ T H I R T Y
-------------
S E V E N T Y
```

February 24

On January 28, you were introduced to word ladders, where one
word is transformed into another by changing one letter at a time
without altering the positions of the other letters, and always
leaving a word at every stage of the process. We saw that FIND
could be transformed into LOSE like this:

FIND
FINE
LINE
LONE
LOSE

Of course, there is nothing to stop you from creating word ladders using words of more than four letters. For example, THINK can be transformed into OPINE like this:

THINK
THANK
THANE
THINE
SHINE
SPINE
OPINE

Perhaps you would care to try your hand at transforming BLACK into WHITE.

February 25

My five grocery items each weighed a whole number of ounces, and the total weight was less than two pounds. With a balance scale, I found the following three inequalities, and in each case, the addition of the banana to the lighter side turned it into the heavier side.

a. tomato and apple together failed to balance the orange
b. apple and orange together failed to balance the potato
c. tomato and orange together failed to balance the potato

I also found the following instances of equality:

d. apple balanced the banana and tomato together
e. tomato and potato together balanced against the other three items together

What was the weight of each item?

February 26

At the last Congressional election in New City, a total of 54,730 votes were cast. The Democrat was elected by a majority of 180 over the Republican, by 1,460 over the Independent, and by 5,750 over the Socialist candidate. Can you give a simple rule for figuring out how many votes were polled for each of the candidates?

February 27

Some months have thirty days. Some months have thirty-one days. How many months have twenty-eight days?

February 28

> Thirty days hath September
> April, June and November.
> All the rest have thirty-one,
> Excepting February alone,
> And that has twenty-eight days clear
> And twenty-nine in each leap year.

So goes the old nursery rhyme. When written out solidly in upper-case type and without a hyphen, the number TWENTYNINE is the only number — repeat, the only number — that consists of . . . . what? If TWENTY-NINE is spelled with a hyphen, what further modification must be made to ensure that it too possesses the property which the unhyphenated version has?

March 1

Following are clues for ten words. Against each clue is an indication of the word's length, and also where the letters MAR occur in the word. See if you can work out what the complete words are.

As an example, if the clue was "an employer" and the letter pattern was MA———R, you should be able to work out that the answer is MASTER.

MAR———	an edge
MAR———	a bird
———MAR	another bird
—MA———R	a dilettante
MAR——————	a saint's feast day, November 11
———MAR—	an abridgement
M———A——R—	a very small painting
—M—AR————	just
—————MAR—	a horrifying experience
——M—A———R	one who exercises authority

March 2

A man went into his local post office, walked up to the lady behind the counter, proffered a dollar, and said, "Give me some 2¢ stamps, ten times as many 1¢ stamps, and the balance in 5¢ stamps." How was this puzzling request met?

March 3

In the list of words below, a number of letters are missing, and these are indicated by asterisks. Each group of missing letters spells out the name of a fish. Can you find the missing fish that will complete the words?

a. em****y	f. de***e
b. ****by	g. f***ing
c. ***ble	h. pol****
d. S****speare	i. s****d
e. sp***ed	j. app*****

March 4

Can you complete the construction of this word square by filling in the missing words? Every word is in common use in English.

```
N E S T L E S
E     R     T
S     A     E
T R A I T O R
L     T     N
E     O     E
S T E R N E R
```

March 5

Proverb of the Day: "A slight inclination of the cranium is as adequate as a spasmodic movement of one optic towards a equine quadruped utterly devoid of any visionary capacity." Well, could *you* put it any better?

March 6

A crowd of spectators had gathered on Pennsylvania Avenue to watch members of the Senate arrive for a particularly critical meeting.

"Who's that?" I asked my neighbor, as a bespectacled figure carrying a rolled umbrella arrived.

"Is it the Majority Leader?"

"Yes," he replied.

"Quite right," chimed in a second spectator. "The Majority Leader it is. Looks grim, doesn't he?"

The first of these speakers makes a point of telling the truth three times out of four, and the second tells the truth four times out of five. What was the probability that the gentleman concerned was in fact the Senate Majority Leader?

March 7

Each of the items shown here represents a familiar word, name, phrase or saying. For example, CCCCCCC should be recognized as The Seven Seas. Now have fun with the others.

a. kingk
   g

b. H
   craft

c. LO head VE
      heels

d. EDalienEN

e. house
   stove

f. suMANn

g. rippe

h. EwD&EdD

i.   GGGG
   M GDDG
     GGGG

j. D
   sole

March 8

March the eighth! A simple date, so a simple puzzle. Rearrange the letters of MARCH to make a common English word. Rearrange the letters of EIGHTH to make another common English word. The names of which other months can have their letters rearranged so as to spell out other words or names?

March 9

Two pieces of metal chain were picked up on the battlefield. Their original purpose is unclear, and, anyway, is of no importance to us here. The chains were formed of circular links, all of the same size, made from metal half an inch thick. One piece of chain was precisely 3 feet long. The other piece was 22 inches. Assuming that one piece of chain contained six links more than the other, how many links were there in each piece of chain?

March 10

As we learned on February 16, a "reversal" is produced when reading a word backward, spells out another, different word. GUM-MUG, RATS-STAR and DEVIL-LIVED were offered as examples of reversals. Given below are six pairs of definitions, each pair corresponding to a pair of reversals. Given in brackets after the definitions are the numbers of letters in the words sought. Can you find all the reversals?

A creature (6)	A ten-pound note (6)
A thin layer (6)	Used for curdling milk (6)
Part of a desk (6)	To hand over (7)
A prize (6)	Hated (7)
A space-bar (6)	Final courses (8)
Goes over again (6)	Emphasized (8)

March 11

The following phrases represent common British inn-names, which should be familiar to all epicures of fine lagers and ales. All contain the name of an animal or a bird. The word THE has been left out of the inn-names. For example, REND OIL would be RED Lion. Do you get the idea? Now try these.

a. He locks bar	d. Bank claws
b. With heroes	e. Choose and crash
c. Gran gone red	f. Wash twine

March 12

A missionary visits an island where two tribes live. One tribe's members always tell the truth. The members of the other tribe always lie. The truth-tellers live on the western side of the island, and the liars live on the eastern side. The missionary's problem is to determine the truth by asking one native only one question.

The missionary, seeing a native walking in the distance, tells a nearby native: "Go ask that native in the distance which side of the island he lives on." When the messenger returns he answers, "He says he lives on the western side."

Is the messenger a truth-teller or a liar? How can you be sure?

March 13

None of the half dozen sentences below makes sense, but they can be made to make sense if you know how. In each sentence, every word of four or more letters can be rearranged to give some other word. Leave all the words in their present order, and that's it! For example, given "Outside suited can diver one to diapers" should be transformed to "Tedious duties can drive one to despair." How many of the sentences can you make sense of?

a. The finished respect unhats the Roman ache thing.
b. Nerve filter whit garnets basset.
c. Ingenue quinate leaders models lead in spiracle.
d. A pierce if prefect slits all the tenderising.
e. A donator can sauce marginal rustles hewn it this a wont.
f. In gleaner tearing corks are the threads nose.

March 14

A different fruit is buried in each of the following lines. Can you spot them?

Ah! If I get my good ship home
I'll find a tempting rural spot,
Where mayhap pleasant flowers will bloom,
And there I'll shape a charming cot.

Where bees sip nectar in each flower,
And Philomel on hawthorn rests
I'll shape a rustic, sun-kissed bower—
A bower meet for angel guests.

Then she who lives and loves with me,
Cheering our days of calm repose,
Sole monarch of the flowers will be —
For Myra is indeed a rose.

March 15

Ides of March

Using just the letters in the phrase IDES OF MARCH, how many girls' and boys' names can you find? Two rather uncommon names are EROS and MICAH, but we're sure you'll be able to unearth some commoner names than those. Remember, no letter may be used more than once in each name.

March 16

A particular type of electronic pocket calculator can handle numbers up to seven digits long. Because of the simple way in which digits are represented, the numbers 0, 1, 2, 5 and 8 read the same either way up, while 6 and 9 read as each other when upside down. This property leads to many intriguing mathematical possibilities. Here is one such poser. What is the smallest number which, when entered and squared, by using the x^2 key, can be read upside down as a different number and its square? Please, no palindromic numbers (such as 11). Nor do we want zero as an answer. We are hoping that you will be able to find a four-digit number meeting the conditions.

March 17

St. Patrick's Day

In the exuberance of his joy at the prospect of becoming a father in his old age, Patrick O'Malley vowed to settle two-thirds of his estate upon 'the boy' and one-third on his own wife, but in case 'the boy' turned out to be a girl, then two-thirds of the estate should go to his wife and one-third to the daughter. However, it turned out that 'the boy' was actually twins, one boy *and* one girl. Of course, this made it necessary for O'Malley to provide for both his offspring as well as his wife. O'Malley, unfortunately, was not in any state to decide on the proper way in which to settle his estate. So, how would you suggest that O'Malley divides his estate?

March 18

During one of the recent currency crises, one particular banker on business in London had a busy time wheeling and dealing in the European financial centers. On Saturday morning, he traveled to Paris where he arranged to dispose of his pounds sterling at the rate of £1 sterling to 3 French francs plus 1 German mark plus 36 Spanish pesetas. The same evening he was in Frankfurt, where he disposed of his marks at the rate of 1 mark to 1 franc plus 12 pesetas. He then went out on the town to celebrate his deals, went to bed very late, got the first plane to Geneva the next morning, and didn't discover until he was actually at the Stock Exchange that the pound sterling had lost one-eighth of its value overnight. So, he exchanged the rest of his pounds at the rate of £1 to 3 francs plus 2 marks, and returned to London. If the only change in currency exchange rates over the weekend was the drop in the value of the pound overnight, how many francs was £1 worth on Saturday morning?

March 19

Take a word of four letters, then add two letters at the end so that the last four letters spell a new word. Add two more letters so that the final four again spell a new word. Repeat this process until you reach a final given word. If, for example, you wanted to change WEST to EAST, you might proceed as follows:

WESTAREAST

The chain of words here is WEST, STAR, AREA and EAST. Now try turning ARMY into NAVY in the same way. All the words used must be English, and avoid proper names such as ANNA and MARY. Oh yes, do try and make the chain as short as possible.

March 20

At my local do-it-yourself center, I was quoted 12 cents for one, 24 cents for 50, and 36 cents for 144. I wanted six. What was I buying, and how much did it cost me?

March 21

If you take all nine of the non-zero digits and place them as follows:

$$\frac{6729}{13458}$$

you will have a fraction equal in value to exactly one-half. Now, can you arrange the nine non-zero digits similarly so as to form fractions exactly equal to one-third, one-quarter, one-fifth, one-sixth, one-seventh, one-eighth, and one-ninth, respectively?

March 22

Three men, traveling with their wives, came to a river. There they found one boat, but it could only carry two people at a time. Since all the husbands are extremely jealous, no woman can be left with a man unless her husband is present. How do they cross the river? You can assume that each man has just one wife, and that each woman has one husband. That helps to keep things wonderfully simple!

March 23

The other day, I found a faded lottery ticket which had got torn in two in an old jacket pocket. The ticket originally bore the number 3025, but had been torn in such a way that the 30 was on one half of the ticket, and the 25 was on the other half. Almost unconsciously, I noticed that if 30 and 25 are added together, and the sum is then squared, the result is the original complete number on the ticket. Thus, 30 plus 25 is 55, and 55 multiplied by itself is 3025. Isn't that odd? Are there any other four-digit numbers, all digits different, that can be treated in the same way? If so, what are they? If not, how do you know?

March 24

What American state does TINA come from? It could be either norTh carolINA or wesT virgINiA, because, as you can see, the girl's name is embedded in the state name with the letters still in the correct sequence. Here are some more names. Can you find their states of origin?

a. Eva   f. Rhoda

b. Mae   g. Diana

c. Alan   h. Sylvia

d. Anton   i. Dean

e. Nesta   j. Sharon

March 25

It is a notorious fact that people's names, like almost any other group of words, can have their letters rearranged so as to form other words. See how easy it is to change MARY into ARMY, or ALEC into LACE, or CAMERON into ROMANCE. How many of the 16 words that follow can you rearrange to successfully find the lady? In a couple of cases, there is more than just one name which can be found — so be warned!

a. dangle	c. bander
b. airman	d. riding
e. bather	k. habitat
f. ethers	l. toaster
g. aimless	m. ailerons
h. retotal	n. ordinals
i. redried	o. senhorita
j. middler	p. redealing

March 26

720 is a remarkable number. It can be divided, without remainder, by lots of other numbers—1, 2, 3, 4, 5, 6, 8, 9, 10, 12, 15, 16, 18, 20, 24, 30, 36, 40, 45, 48, 60, 72, 80, 90, 120, 144, 180, 240, 360, and 720. That's 30 different numbers in all. But can you find an even more remarkable number, less than 1000, one that can be divided by 32 different numbers which leave no remainders? There is one such number. How long will it take you to discover it?

March 27

A gentleman who died recently left *just over* $8000 to be divided between his widow, his five sons, and four daughters. He stipulated that every son should receive three times as much as a daughter, and that every daughter should receive twice as much as their mother. If the precise amount left by the man was $7999.97 (notice that the figures read the same backward as forward), how much did the widow receive?

March 28

Two or more successive words in each of these sentences are a rearrangement of the name of a famous person to whom the sentence refers. Hint: the four names refer to five people, including two scientists, a mathematician, an artist, an old philosopher, a silent film star, and a film star of the 1970's!

a. He often walked a lone road, years ahead of his time.
b. From apples he went on to mints.
c. He tore a slit in the veil of our ignorance.
d. No one could take on the role of this funny and amusing person.

March 29

A customer went into a pet shop and bought two rabbits plus half the remaining rabbits. A second customer went into the shop and bought three rabbits plus one-third of the remaining rabbits. A third customer went into the shop and bought four rabbits plus one-quarter of the remaining rabbits. And so on, until it was no longer possible to continue without splitting rabbits. How many customers went away satisfied?

March 30

What English word in common use will describe a person or thing as not to be found in any place whatever, and yet, with no alteration other than a mere space between the syllables, will correctly describe that person or thing as being actually present at this very moment?

When you have found the word concerned, rearrange its letters to form two other words.

March 31

We saw on February 20 that certain words can be turned into apt descriptions of themselves by skillful rearrangement of the letters comprising the words. We saw that ENDEARMENTS applied most fittingly to TENDER NAMES, and that INCOMPREHENSIBLES could well be PROBLEMS IN CHINESE. Such apposite letter re-arrangements we called "anagrams." Given below are 6 anagrams. Your task is to reconstruct the six original words which were scrambled to produce these anagrams. Remember that in each case, you are required to turn the given phrase into just one appropriate word.

a. Mystics in a heap
b. Our men earn it
c. Life's aim
d. A stern sense
e. Seen as mist

April 1

April Fools' Day

A man runs *n* times around a circular track whose radius is *t* miles. He drinks *s* quarts of beer for every mile that he runs. Prove that he will need only one quart. (Just in case your mathematics is somewhat rusty, the circumference of a circle is obtained by multiplying 2. pi by the radius.)

April 2

In this limerick, which concerns a young man of limited mental ability, all the A's, P's, R's, I's and L's have been omitted, nearly 50 in all. Can you replace them?

vte te on de
ceessy shoudeed sde
ced sge stnd t ese
esent ms f you ese
vet Gss hs new knd of bde!

April 3

On March 25 you saw how easy it was to rearrange feminine first-names so as to make other words. Names of cities can be juggled in the same way. A couple of examples: PARIS can be transformed into PAIRS quite easily, and LAS VEGAS becomes SALVAGES. How many of the 16 words given below can you rearrange successfully so as to find the cities?

a. hasten   i. reddens
b. planes   j. romance
c. animal   k. nerved
d. gainer   l. dottier
e. granite   m. grained
f. angriest   n. diagnose
g. testier   o. rechewing
h. Juanita   p. relanding

April 4

From certain single observations, it is possible to draw two-pronged conclusions. For example, from the observation "He tipped his mortarboard to a lady," it could be concluded that "He's a gentleman and a scholar." For the five observations given here, can you furnish suitable double conclusions?

a. I bought an asbestos canoe
b. He's wallowing in his huge guano beds
c. Clad in armour, he threw his wallet into the San Andreas Rift
d. I saw the girl clutching an empty magnum of brut champagne
e. Miss America turned down the cardiac patient

April 5

In the following multiplication, each letter stands for a different digit. Can you substitute digits for letters so as to end up with a "correct" multiplication?

```
        L Y N D O N
X               B
        J O H N S O N
```

April 6

Dwight had been playing cards with three of his friends. Thinking about the game afterwards, he recalled these facts:

a. Ambrose and Bertram had better scores than the doctor
b. Ambrose first dealt to Bertram, then to Mr. Hooper, then to the accountant, and then to himself
c. In the last hand, Bertram dealt to the priest, to Mr. Hooper, to Clint, and then to himself
d. Mr. Eastwood went home before Clint did
e. The doctor had a better score than Mr. Grimm
f. Mr. Fuller went home before the priest

With these facts, sprinkled with a little logical deduction, you ought to be able to work out who was who. For example, what were the musician's first and last names?

April 7

William Wordsworth's birthday (1770)

Wandering, through many a year, 'mongst Cumbria's hills,
  O'er her wild fells, sweet vales, and sunny lakes,
Rich stores of thought thy musing mind distils,
  Daydreams of poesy thy soul awakes —
Such was thy life — a poet's life, I ween;
  Worshipper thou of Nature! every scene
Of beauty stirred thy fancy's deeper mood
  Reflection calmed the current of thy blood:

Thus in the wide excursion of thy mind,
    High thoughts in words of worth we still may find.

These lines are unmistakably concerned with Wordsworth. Why?

April 8

A chessboard measures eight squares by eight squares, containing 32 small black squares and 32 small white squares. However, a chessboard may be thought of as being made up of larger squares and rectangles, all composed of the smaller black and white squares. Can you determine just how many squares and rectangles a chessboard does contain? In other words, in how great a number of different ways is it possible to trace out a square or other rectangle enclosed by lines that separate the squares of the board?

April 9

A student of arithmetic learned that the same quantity could be cancelled from the numerator and denominator of a fraction. (The numerator is the top part, and the denominator is the bottom part.) After learning this, when presented with the fraction $\frac{139}{695}$, he cancelled both the 9's, getting $\frac{13}{65}$, or $\frac{1}{5}$. This happened to be correct, but, as his teacher pointed out, "That was an accident. It won't happen again."

The next day, the student returned with another fraction of the same type. He cancelled digits from the same positions as before, and again got the correct result. But his teacher expostulated, "You haven't been consistent. Why didn't you cancel *all* equal digits in the numerator and denominator? Then the result would certainly have been wrong." So the student proceeded to cancel the "units" digit of the numerator and the "tens" digit of the denominator; lo and behold, his teacher was right. What was the second fraction?

April 10

On January 30, we celebrated the birthday of Sam Loyd, probably our greatest puzzle setter. His British counterpart was Henry Dudeney, whose ability to invent entertaining puzzles and present them to the public in attractive ways turned him into one of the first full-time professional puzzle-makers. To celebrate Dudeney's birthday, try this little problem.

A man went into his local bank to cash a check. In handing over the money, the girl behind the counter mistakenly gave him dollars for cents and cents for dollars. The man pocketed the money without even bothering to examine it. On the way home, he spent a nickel. He then found that he possessed exactly twice the amount for which his check had been made out. If he had no money in his pocket before going to the bank, can you tell how much his check was for?

April 11

Below are 20 wrecked cars, some current models, and some seldom seen in working order. Can you untangle the names and present us with a list of 20 unbattered cars?

a. is a nut	k. noticer
b. yellow E's	l. neutral
c. irate Sam	m. the clover
d. lost rib	n. bus name
e. sorry cello	o. solo limbed
f. tow jet	p. not Martians
g. imp hurt first pie	q. vandal pens
h. daunts	r. I'm in
i. coster	s. entrail
j. co-train	t. red mail

41

April 12

In describing her experiences at the winter sales, Mrs. Jones said that half her money was gone in the first hour, so that she was left with as many cents as she had dollars before, and only half as many dollars as before she had cents. So, how much did she spend at the sales?

April 13

On February 19, we came across a word square composed of five five-letter words:

```
C H E S T
H A S T E
E S H E R
S T E E R
T E R R Y
```

Can you solve the following five clues? Taking the words in order should give you another word square.

a. To be wounded
b. Seaport in Northern Ireland
c. Destroy by slow consumption
d. Terminated
e. Exploits

April 14

The names of some countries incorporate a boy's name or a girl's name, with complete and uninterrupted letters. ADA, for instance, appears in both Canada and Grenada. Which countries include the following names in the same way?

a. Guy	d. Dan	g. Gary
b. Eric	e. Don	h. Rita
c. Stan	f. Alan	i. Philip

April 15

Consider the word COLD. If you shift each of the four letters forward three positions in the alphabet, so that C becomes F, O becomes R, L becomes O, and D becomes G, you end up with a new word, FROG. Similarly, BALK can be turned into ONYX by shifting each of the letters forward 13 positions in the alphabet. Now, what we have done is to take ten five-letter words and change them into other words by shifting their letters forward some suitable distance in the alphabet. How rapidly can you work backwards from the words given here and determine what words we started with?

a. beefs	f. ferns	
b. ingot	g. jolly	
c. lorry	h. toffs	
d. sorry	i. tiffs	
e. Freud	j. tiger	

April 16

The ten words and terms given here all rhyme with OH, and yet each ends with a different letter of the alphabet.

dough	woe	oho
whoa	de trop	apropos
sol	row	bon mot
gateaux		

Now, can you find as many words and terms as possible, ending with different letters of the alphabet, that rhyme with the word SAY? You should be able to manage ten or more.

April 17

A problem which crops up quite often in puzzle literature is that of inserting mathematical signs wherever one cares to between the digits 1, 2, 3, 4, 5, 6, 7, 8, and 9 to make the resulting expression equal in value to 100. The digits must remain in the same sequence. One of the numerous solutions to this problem is:

$$1 + 2 + 3 + 4 + 5 + 6 + 7 + (8 \times 9) = 100$$

The problem becomes slightly more difficult if only plus and minus signs are allowed. A typical solution to the problem now is this:

$$12 + 3 - 4 + 5 + 67 + 8 + 9 = 100$$

In this solution, six plus and minus signs were used. Can you find a solution to this plus-and-minus-only problem using as few signs as possible?

April 18

How well do you know film titles? If we were to give you this sequence of vowels and dashes: $--E--I--$, would you be able to fill in the missing consonants and arrive at THE STING? Try your hand at the following ones, all the films being taken from the 1960's and 1970's.

a. $A - E - I - A - - - A - - I - I$
b. $- - I - A - O - -$
c. $- O - - IE A - - - - Y - E$
d. $- O - - E - - A - -$
e. $- - A - - A - -$
f. $- - E E - O - - I - -$

44

g. --E-AY-E-E-E
h. -A-U--AY-I----E-E-
i. --A--OO
j. --E--EA--A---Y

April 19

Eon, two, ether, flour, verify, fixes, evens, weight, inner, net, leavened, wavelet, tethering, counterfeit, stiffener, existent, retentiveness, heightened, internecine, noteworthy. These 20 words are given in a definite, logical order. What is that order? What is the logic behind the words in the list? Is it possible to add further words to the list? If so, specify a few; if not, say why not.

April 20

I have two eggtimers. One takes seven minutes for the sand in the top half to run through to the bottom half, and the other takes eleven minutes. How can I use the two to obtain hardboiled eggs that have been boiled for exactly a quarter of an hour? One way of doing this is as follows. Start both the eggtimers together. When the seven-minute timer runs out, put the eggs into boiling water. When the eleven-minute timer runs out (four minutes later), start the eleven-minute timer again. When it runs out again, the eggs will have boiled for four minutes plus eleven minutes, a quarter of an hour in total. Unfortunately, I have to spend 22 minutes to get these 15-minute eggs. Can you see how I could spend less time in boiling the eggs for 15 minutes?

April 21

Why is the letter D like a hoop of gold?
Why is the letter F like a cow's tail?

Why is the letter T like Easter?

Which two letters are definitely not hard?

April 22

On April 17, we looked at the problem of inserting plus and minus signs between the digits 1, 2, 3, 4, 5, 6, 7, 8, and 9 to make a mathematical expression equal in value to 100. Now, how about the reverse problem? One solution, which uses seven signs altogether, is this:

$$98 + 7 - 6 + 5 - 4 + 3 - 2 - 1 = 100$$

Can you create a solution using fewer plus and minus signs than this? Don't forget that the numbers must stay in the reverse order from 9 down to 1.

April 23

Anniversay of William Shakespeare's death (1616)

Someone once noticed that the letters of WILLIAM SHAKE-SPEARE could be rearranged to form the question I ASK ME, HAS WILL A PEER? Perhaps you would care to juggle with the letters of the Bard's name and see if you can devise a particularly apt anagram, one that has some connection with Shakespeare. Also, as it is St. George's Day too, maybe you would care to wrestle with the phrase SAINT GEORGE AND THE DRAGON, and see if you can invent an anagrammatic statement of some relevance to this particular twosome.

April 24

Idly fingering the office stamp, which is one of those rotating devices which will print out any of a dozen words, I noticed that one word stood out a mile. It was very different from the other eleven words. Which was it and why? The dozen words were:

AIRMAIL	CHECKED	CLASS
CONFIDENTIAL	COPY	FIRST
PAID	RECEIVED	RECORDED
REGISTERED	SECOND	URGENT

April 25

Take the word SPARKLING. Take away any one letter so as to leave a new word. Take away any one letter from the new word so as to leave another new word. Continue to do this, letter by letter, until you finish up with just a single letter. After removing a letter, you must not disturb the order of the remaining letters.

April 26

On April 18, we looked at some films. We asked you to complete various film titles from just the vowels in the names of the films. Here are ten more you might like to attempt.

a. — U — — I — —
b. — E — — O — —
c. E A — — — — U A — E
d. A — — I E — A — —
e. — U — — — E — O O —
f. — — E — O — E — I — — I — — E — — O
g. — — E — — — — O — — E — — I O —
h. — — E — O O —, — — E — A — A — — — — E
   U — — Y
i. — U — — — — A — — I — Y A — — — — E
   — U — — A — — E — I —
j. — — O — E E — — O U — — E — — O —
   — — E — — I — — — I — —

April 27

A boy who enjoys watching trains likes to walk to a railway bridge near his home and wait for a train to go by. Two trains go past each hour. After seeing the first train, he returns home and makes a note of whether it was a passenger train or a goods train. Over the years, his figures show that 90 percent of the trains have been passenger trains. One day he meets a railway worker and is surprised to learn that passenger trains and goods trains are precisely equal in number. Why did the boy, whom we may presume to have made random trips to the railway bridge, see such a disproportionate number of passenger trains?

April 28

Just for a change, here are some answers:

a. About 30 drachmas a week
b. No strings attached
c. Crick
d. Chromatic scales
e. A youthful figure
f. A Greek letter
g. Carbon 14, uranium 235
h. Around the word in 80 days

All right — now you provide the questions having these answers.

April 29

Three goats graze on a fenced-in meadow containing 120 square yards in the shape of an equal-sided triangle. Each goat is tethered to a stake set in a different corner of the meadow and the tethers are just long enough for a goat to reach the middle of the opposite fence. If you consider that a goat grazes all the area he alone can reach, half the area shared by two goats alone, and one-third of the area commonly grazed by all three, how much area in all does one goat graze?

April 30

A pack of 52 playing cards (no jokers) is divided by cutting into two unequal portions. If a card is drawn randomly from one portion, the odds are 2 to 1 against its being a red card. A red card is next transferred from the other portion to the first portion. Now the odds are 2 to 1 against a card drawn randomly from the second portion being black. How was the pack originally divided?

May 1

May Day

Below are clues for ten words. Against each clue is an indication of the word's length, and also where the letters MAY occur in the word. See if you can work out what the complete words are. As an example, if the clue was "international distress signal" and the letter pattern was MAY———, you should be able to work out that the answer is MAYDAY.

MAY — — —	malicious damage
MAY — — — — — —	seasoned sauce
— — — MAY	discourage
— — MA — Y	gypsy
M — — — AY	a day of the week
MA — — — Y	the Thursday before Good Friday
— M — A — — Y	an ambassador's residence
M — A — Y	spotty
— MA — — — Y	relating to love
— M — — — — A — — Y	augustly

49

May 2

On February 19 and April 13, we came across word squares using five different five-letter words. Now is your chance to meet a word square using six different six-letter words. Just solve the six clues given below. The six answers, taken in order, will form the word square.

a. parent's right to see a child
b. close-fitting inner garment
c. hole in the ground
d. a housing development
e. to boil
f. a public road

May 3

Consider the names of all the numbers from ONE to ONE BILLION. If all one billion of those names were arranged in alphabetical order, which of them would be first, and which would be last? Before you begin to work on this problem, you must realize that a name such as BILLION is not a valid name; we are only interested in full names, such as ONE BILLION or FOUR HUNDRED AND EIGHT MILLION TWO HUNDRED AND TWENTY-NINE THOUSAND EIGHT HUNDRED AND THIRTY-FIVE. Furthermore, because of the difference between the American-French and the British-German systems of notation, we must define precisely what we mean by the number ONE BILLION. ONE BILLION is to be understood to be equal to one thousand million, that is, a 1 followed by nine 0's.

May 4

The biologist Thomas Huxley is generally credited with having first made the often-repeated statement that if you set six monkeys at six typewriters they would *eventually* write the works of Shakespeare. Huxley was illustrating the role of chance in the evolutionary process. Well, then, if a monkey set at a typewriter strikes each of the 26 upper-case letters once, and only once, what is the probability that somewhere in the random array four successive letters will spell, left to right, the names IAGO or LEAR?

May 5

What is the missing number in this arrangement?

1	2	3	4	5
1	3	9	21	41
1	4	31	220	1081
1	5	129	6949	?

May 6

How well do you know the titles of novels? If we were to give you this sequence of vowels and dashes: — — E I — — I — I — — E — A —, would you be able to fill in the missing consonants and arrive at THE INVISIBLE MAN? Try your hand at the following ones.

a. — A — I — Y — AI —
b. — O — — A — — — O — E — —
c. — I — — O — A — — I — — — E — Y
d. — U — — — E — E — — Y — I — —
e. — A — — — E — I — — — E — YE
f. A — U — — O — IA — — O — IA — I — —
g. A — I — A — — A — —
h. U — Y — — E —
i. — O — I — A
j. — — — O

May 7

Ahoy, blow, chin, defy, erst, flux, gist, hint, imps, know, lops, most. Twelve reasonably common words. Apart from all having four letters, what do they have in common? Can you provide us with a five-letter word having the same property? And a six-letter one?

May 8

A man went into a bank with exactly $1000, all in dollar bills. He gave the money to a cashier and said, "Put this money into ten bags in such a way that if I call and ask for a certain number of dollars, you can hand me over one or more bags, giving me the exact amount called for, without having to open any of the bags."

How was the cashier to do this?

May 9

You have an electronic pocket calculator, which has nine display positions. Accordingly, it is capable of displaying a nine-digit integer or an eight-digit number involving a decimal point. Anyway, here are ten simple sums which you decide to work out using your calculator. What is the significance of the answers? What hidden meaning do they possess? If you don't see any hidden meaning at first, try looking at the answers from a different perspective.

a. $(366 \times 10) + (2 \times 2 \times 11)$
b. $(366 \times 15) + (2 \times 2 \times 55)$
c. $(366 \times 16) - 123$
d. $(366 \times 19) + (3 \times 17) + 100$
e. $(366 \times 20) + (20 \times 20) - 4$
f. $(366 \times 21) + 148$

g. $(230 \times 230) + (366 \times 2) + 119$

h. $(366 \times 867) + 215$

i. $(366 \times 2) - 22 + \frac{3}{4} + 0.02345$

j. $(366 \times 10.002) + 44.0414$

May 10

We saw on February 20, March 31 and April 23 that certain words can be turned into apt descriptions or explanations of themselves by a skillful rearrangement of the letters comprising the words. We saw that ENDEARMENTS is a word that applies most fittingly to TENDER NAMES, and a good example of INCOMPREHEN-SIBLES is provided by PROBLEMS IN CHINESE. Such apposite rearrangements were called anagrams.

It is also possible to turn a word into its own *opposite*, produc-ing what is known as an 'antigram'. For example, EVANGELISTS can be transformed into EVIL'S AGENTS, and DESECRATION can be changed into the opposite-meaning CONSIDERATE. Listed below are antigrams created from six single-word sub-jects. Can you figure out for each the one word that is a fitting antigram?

a. Nice to imports

b. Nice love

c. Archsaints

d. Fine tonic

e. I limit arms

f. Is it legal? No!

May 11

Typically, the professor was very absent-minded. However, he never forgot the number of his house. Apart from having three digits, it possessed the following unusual property: the sum of all the house numbers in the street less than it equalled the sum of all the house numbers in the street that exceeded it. Unfortunately, this won't be true for much longer because the local council are about to bulldoze several old houses to make way for a recreation ground, but at the moment all the houses are present. Just what is the number of the professor's house then?

May 12

Dante Gabriel Rossetti's birthday (1828)

On April 23, William Shakespeare's birthday, we saw that his name could be anagrammed into the phrase "I ask me, has Will a peer?" Perhaps you would care to search for an apposite anagram on the name of DANTE GABRIEL ROSSETTI, the English painter and poet. See how your anagrams measure up to the one in the answers section.

May 13

An officer wishing to arrange his men in a solid square found by his first arrangement that he had 39 men over. He then started increasing the number of men on a side by one, but found that 50 additional men would be needed to complete the new square. How many men did the officer have?

May 14

A glass is one-third full of wine. Another glass, with equal capacity, is only one-quarter full of wine. Each glass is then filled to the brim with water, and the contents of both glasses are poured into a jug. Half of the mixture is poured into one of the glasses. What proportion of the wine and what proportion of the water are now in this glass?

May 15

When an expert burlesque queen named Maizy,
Stripping velvet, became very lazy,
She would quickly exhibit
Just one jeweled explicit,
Gliding off from the jokesters like crazy.

What special quality does this limerick possess?

May 16

Army, chat, fish, girl, horn, knit, soup, swan, vote. Nine cards
bearing the words above are placed face up on a table. Alternately,
you and an imaginary opponent draw cards. The object is to
obtain three which share a common letter, the first player doing
this being the winner. The toss of an imaginary coin gives your
opponent the advantage of the first move. He promptly takes the
card bearing the word "knit." How should you continue?

May 17

A man can walk up a moving "up" escalator in 30 seconds. He can
walk down this moving "up" escalator in 1-½ minutes. If his walking pace is the same going upstairs as downstairs, how long would
it take him to climb the escalator if it was stationary? How long
would it take him to go up the moving escalator if he stood still?

May 18

On January 28 and February 25, we came across word ladders,
where one word is transformed into another by changing one

letter at a time without altering the positions of the other letters, and always leaving a word at every stage of the process. We saw that FIND could be transformed into LOSE like this:

FIND
FINE
LINE
LONE
LOSE

Can you find ladders for the following transformations?

a. EAST to WEST
b. HATE to LOVE
c. HEAT to FIRE
d. LEAD to GOLD
e. LION to BEAR
f. DUSK through DARK to DAWN

May 19

A man ordered a length of rope by telephone from his nearest hardware shop. But when he went to collect the rope, he found that the assistant had miswritten the order by interchanging feet and inches. As a result of this, the rope was only 30 percent of the length that the man wanted. So, what length did he want and what length did he get?

May 20

Each of the sentences given here conceals a familiar abbreviation, the letters appearing together and in their proper order. For example, "Terrorist group aims gun at other side" conceals NATO in the fourth, fifth and sixth words.

a. We hope cigarette taxes don't rise as quickly as the price of gas did.
b. Bess Myerson made her attitude toward female politicians famous.
c. We pay taxes to keep our air and water clean.
d. They used the moon as a first step for space exploration.
e. Farmers consider it an odd time for spraying.

May 21

Each of the following phrases suggests a well-known town or city. For example, "Second Sibling" is really "Tucson." How many of the 10 below can you solve?

a. Neophyte covener
b. Coronary crossing
c. Breakable bovine
d. Summon the knifer
e. Angrily disencumber
f. A friend of mine
g. Novel boat
h. Regal heavyweight
i. Impoverished vocalizer
j. Two in the present tense
k. Stylishly leaving

May 22

Wayne treated his girlfriend to a bus ride, but on account of his limited resources they had to walk back. Now, if the bus goes at an average speed of 9 miles per hour and they walk back at the rate of three miles per hour, how far can they ride so that they can be back in eight hours?

May 23

It's common knowledge that food can be presented in a variety of different ways. For example, PARSLEY can have its letters re-arranged so that it is presented as PLAYERS; and BROTHS can be presented as THROBS. Given here are a dozen foods, presented in a variety of ways. Can you untangle the letters and arrive back at the foods we started with?

a. trance   g. assuage

b. unpaste   h. aridness

c. unstrip   i. harmonicas

d. scuttle   j. segregates

e. chariot   k. mentioners

f. orblets   l. solemn

May 24

Find the seven missing initials of the six-letter words given below, and they will spell out a proper noun. When you get it, try again. You may be able to find a similar object.

—U M B L E

—M P I R E

—A T T E R

—O N I C S

—R I N A L

—A S T E R

—A R E L Y

May 25

A census taker asked a housewife how many people lived in her house and what their ages were. The woman told him that her three daughters lived in the house, that the product of their ages was 36, and that the sum of their ages was the number of the house next door. The census taker went next door and looked at the number on the door. When he returned, he told the housewife that the information she had given him was insufficient, whereupon she replied, "My oldest daughter is sleeping upstairs." The census taker thanked her and promptly figured out the daughters' ages. What were they and how did he know?

May 26

In each of the following statements is hidden the name of a country. For example, in the sentence "His painstaking efforts were much admired," the name of SPAIN is hidden in the first two words. Can you find the six hidden countries?

a. The only animal I've ever owned was a nice eland.
b. Every newspaper understands the responsibilities it has towards its readers.
c. The cha-cha, it is a dance, as is the bossa nova.
d. When having a bonfire, check that all gas is safely out of the way.
e. Hoots mon! A comet fell in a Scottish county yesterday.
f. Interpol and the FBI are working together on the giant fraud case.

May 27

The combined ages of Mark and Andrew are 44, and Mark is twice as old as Andrew was when Mark was half as old as Andrew will be when Andrew is three times as old as Mark was when Mark was three times as old as Andrew. How old is Mark? If you cannot work it out, ask your friends to help you, and watch the bewilderment creep over their faces as they attempt to grapple with the problem.

May 28

Using the musical notes C, D, E, F, G, A and B, what is the longest word that can be played on the piano? That is, using some or all of these letters, as many or as few times as you like, what is the longest word you can find? No foreign or hyphenated words, please.

May 29

QWERTYUIOP are the letters on the top row of letters on a standard typewriter keyboard. What is the longest word that can be typed using just those letters? You may start off with words like QUIRE, PEPPER and TORTURE, but you'll probably end up with ones longer than these.

May 30

Yesterday we asked you to find the longest word that could be typed with the top row of letters on a standard typewriter. Today, what is the longest word that can be typed using the next row of letters on a standard typewriter: ASDFGHJKL?

May 31

On April 3, we saw that the names of various cities and towns around the world could have their letters rearranged so as to spell other words. For example, PARIS became PAIRS and LAS VEGAS became SALVAGES.

Our universities and colleges, and their hometowns, are just as susceptible to this kind of letter juggling as foreign placenames. To make this a little tougher, try to unscramble the names of the colleges and universities + hometowns given below in word series. An example is THIN, ARC, NO, CALL = Cornell, Ithaca.

a. SEW, RENT, RUBS, WICK, RUNG

b. HEN, WAVEY, LEAN

c. ANNUAL, SWORE, LENT

d. HAM, KUDU, RED

e. CLAD, FIG, CRIB, FRAME

f. SO, PAUPER, GIVES, SHAKE

June 1

Below are clues for ten words. Against each clue is an indication of the word's length, and also where the letters JUN occur in the word. See if you can sort out what the complete words are. As an example, if the clue was "an evergreen coniferous shrub" and the letter pattern was JUN — — E —, you should be able to work out that the answer is JUNIPER.

JUN — — E	dense tropical forest
JUN — E —	a feast, picnic or spree
J — U — NE —	an excursion
JU — — N — — E	pertaining to youth
J — U — N — — E — —	newspaper or magazine jargon
JUN — E — — — —	large, buxom and beautiful
JU — — — — — — — N — E	knowledge of the law
— — JUN — — — — E	forming an additional, subordinate part
JUN — — — — E	an important point
— — J — UNE —	French for breakfast or lunch

June 2

TWO × TWO = THREE

Each letter stands for one and only one digit, and no digit is represented by more than one letter. Can you work out what digits the letters in the above multiplication stand for so that the identity above is actually correct?

June 3

Someone once suggested that the word WORD could well be considered as a *W*ritten *O*ffering *R*eadily *D*efined, the initial letters spelling out WORD and the whole phrase defining the word WORD. Along the same lines, can you devise similar phrases for the following words: letters, anagram, alphabet, palindrome, and acronym? Remember, the initial letters in each phrase must spell out the word being defined, and the whole definition must be relevant.

June 4

Here is a passage of five lines taken from a famous poem:

"Oft on autumnal eves, when without in the gathering darkness
Bursting with light seemed the smithy, through every cranny and crevice,
Warm by the forge within they watched the labouring bellows,
And as its panting ceased, and the sparks expired in the ashes,
Merrily laughed, and said they were nuns going into the chapel."

Can you identify the poem from which these lines are taken, and its author? There is something astonishing about one of the lines. Which one, and what is it?

June 5

A clock takes exactly two seconds to strike two o'clock. How long will it take to strike three o'clock?

June 6

A month ago, on May 6, we quizzed you on novel titles. If you recall, we gave you just the vowels in the titles of various novels, and asked you to identify the novels. For example, $--$E I$--$I$-$I$--$E$-$A$-$ should be recognizable as THE INVISIBLE MAN. Now try your hand at the following ones.

a. $--$E A$--$I$-$A$--$E$--$I$---$O$-$
b. $-$A$---$E$--$E$--$O$-$E$--$
c. $-$A$--$E$-$Y$-$O$-$
d. $---$E$-$Y$--$A$-----$Y$-$E
e. E$--$I$---$OO$-$
f. $--$O$--$U$--$IA$-$I$---$O$-$E
g. $-$UY$-$A$--$E$-$I$--$
h. $-$I$---$E$-$O$-$E$-$
i. $-$O$-$I$---$AY
j. U$-$O$-$IA

June 7

As usual, there were well over 100 people at the orgy. Exactly as many were in favor of playing Postman's Knock as were against, so Lawrence proposed playing Strip Liar Dice. This time, 52 percent of the voters were in favor since 13 more people voted for Dice than Postman's Knock. Allan, who was still sober, immediately remarked that the ratio of votes in favor for the two games was the inverse of the ratio against. What was the voting for each game?

June 8

Three intelligent men, applying for a job, seem equal in all relevant attributes, so the prospective employer, also an intelligent man, sets a simple problem for them. He declares that the job will go to the first applicant correctly solving the problem. A mark is placed on each applicant's forehead. The three are then told that each has either a black mark or a white mark on his forehead. Each is to raise his hand if he sees a black mark on the forehead of either of the other two. The first one to tell correctly the color of the mark on his own forehead, and how he has arrived at the answer, will get the job. Each man raises his hand, and after a few seconds, one man comes up with the correct answer. What color is his mark, and how did he figure it out?

June 9

NICHOLAS NICKLEBY was one of Charles Dickens' novels, concerned with the life and adventures of Nicholas Nickleby. Perhaps you would care to juggle with the letters of that last phrase (THE LIFE AND ADVENTURES OF NICHOLAS NICKLEBY) and see if you can devise a particularly apt anagram, one having some relevance to the author.

June 10

Find, if you can, a reasonable explanation for the pairing of the following words.

AIL and PAIN   COURT and MAIN
SALE and FOUR   COIN and DENT
OR and PAYS   SABLE and TOUR
TON and CHOSE   BOND and AN
CHAMP and BUT   OURS and CHAT

June 11

A man planted two poles upright in level ground. One pole was
6ft. 6in. and the other 7ft. 7in. above ground. From the top of
each pole he tied a string to the bottom of the other, just where it
entered the ground. Now, what height above the ground was the
point where the two strings crossed? You may be wondering why
we have neglected to tell you how far apart the two poles are.
Their distance of separation is of no consequence. Two feet or
two hundred feet, it will not affect the answer.

June 12

Put three letters in front of and the same three letters (in the same
order) behind each of the following groups of letters so as to form
words.

ERTAINM
ENTIALN
ERGRO
ACHA
SH
AU
X

June 13

I am a word of 12 letters.
My 12, 4, 7, 2, 5 is an Eastern beast of burden.
My 1, 8, 10, 9 is a street made famous by Sinclair Lewis.
My 11, 3, 6 is past.
My whole is a person suffering from delusions of greatness.
So, who am I?

June 14

Flag Day

To celebrate Flag Day, can you figure out what this letter sequence might represent?

$$O - CY - BTDEL - - P - H$$

What letters are missing?

June 15

Mrs. Murphy wanted some oranges, so she sent Margaret to the corner shop to get them. Margaret came back a few minutes later with some oranges and six lollipops, having spent a total of 43 cents. Unfortunately, she didn't buy enough oranges, so her brother Mike was sent to get some more. He returned soon after, also with some oranges and seven sticks of toffee, having spent the same amount as his sister. What are the prices of the oranges, the lollipops, and the toffee sticks? Each item costs a whole number of cents, and all the items are realistically priced.

June 16

Here is another word square puzzle like that met on May 2. Solve the following six clues. The six answers, each of six letters, will form a word square when taken in order.

a. does wrong to
b. commotion
c. extortionist

d. struggled vigorously
e. team
f. calm

June 17

I am a word of 11 letters.
My 7, 3, 8, 4, 5 is what the little girl did when her cat died.
My 9, 10, 6, 2 is an obscuring smudge.
My 1, 11 is an abbreviation for that is.
My whole is as little as it can get.
What am I?

June 18

Peter Piper picked a peck of pickled peppers, but how long did it take him? We know that Peter and his friend Paul, working together, could pick a peck in 20 minutes; Paul and his friend Percival, working together, could do the job in 30 minutes. Peter and Percival working together, though, would take 40 minutes to pick a peck. So, just how long would it take for Peter to pick a peck of pickled peppers by himself?

June 19

Five hundred begins it, five hundred ends it,
Five in the middle is seen;
The first of all figures, the first of all letters,
Take up their stations between.
Join all together, and then you will bring
Before you the name of an eminent king.

June 20

This may look the same as the puzzle presented on January 20, but it isn't. Below are 25 letters of the alphabet, omitting the Q. Starting at any one of the letters and moving one letter at a time up or down or left or right or diagonally, see how many different words you can spell out. Words should have at least three letters. No word may use a letter more than once. And no proper names, foreign words, abbreviations and plurals, please. Can you find more than 20 words?

```
A B C D E
J I H G F
K L M N O
U T S R P
V W X Y Z
```

June 21

PACK MY BOX WITH FIVE DOZEN LIQUOR JUGS is an understandable sentence of 32 letters containing all 26 letters of the alphabet, the extra 6 letters all being vowels. Can you find a sentence using all alphabetical letters twice, with any extra letters being vowels? Can you beat the 71-letter example that we have unearthed?

June 22

Dictionaries define words in terms of other words. If we look up these other words, we are treated to yet other words; and so on. This permits us to build a chain of synonymous words. If we do this carefully and schemingly, unforeseen results are likely to follow; unforeseen to the ordinary dictionary user, anyway. Consider the case of BLACK. Dictionary investigation yields a series of equalities revealing to us that black really is white. Thus:

black = dark	snug = comfortable
dark = obscure	comfortable = easy
obscure = hidden	easy = simple
hidden = concealed	simple = pure
concealed = snug	pure = white

The turning point is, of course, the pairing of CONCEALED, a word with negative associations, with SNUG, a word with positive associations. Since dictionaries equate the two words, so do we. In the same way, can you prove that UGLY is really BEAUTI-FUL? And can you identify where the switch from bad to good takes place in your chain?

June 23

The letters of the alphabet can be grouped into four distinct classes. The first 13 letters establish the categories:

A M

B C D E K

F G J L

H I

Place the remaining 13 letters in their proper categories.

June 24

Midsummer's Day

Puck in *A Midsummer Night's Dream* said that he would put a girdle round about the earth in 40 minutes. Let us suppose that the earth is a perfect sphere with a smooth surface, and a girdle of steel is placed round the equator so that it touches at every point. Now suppose that it is decided to add 6 yards to the length of the steel girdle. What then will be the distance between the girdle and the earth, assuming that the distance around the earth is the same? Do you think that such a small addition will have any noticeable effect bearing in mind that the earth's equator measures approximately 25,000 miles?

June 25

What is the smallest square number that ends with the greatest possible number of identical digits? Thus, the greatest possible number might be five and the smallest square number with five identical digits at the end might be 12377777. But this is certainly not a square number. Zero, of course, is not to be considered as a digit in this little puzzle.

June 26

a. Why is a crossword puzzle like a quarrel?
b. Why are riddles that cannot be answered like a man disappointed by his visitors?
c. What letter is most useful to a deaf person?
d. Why is a bad cold like a great humiliation?
e. Why is a schoolboy being flogged like your eye?
f. What time is when the clock strikes thirteen?
g. What is black and white and red all over?
h. What occurs once in a minute, twice in a moment, but not once in a hundred years?
i. What ship has two mates but no captain?
j. Why is a person reading these puzzles like a man condemned to undergo military execution?

June 27

Bus conductors occasionally have to put up with more than the mere offer of a dollar bill for the fare to the next stop. Consider this exchange between the awkward passenger and the sharp bus conductor.

"Times Square, please," said the passenger.

"Where did you get on?"

"Two stops after the stop which is one stop less than halfway to Times Square," announced the passenger, pleased with himself.

The conductor thought for a moment, and replied, "The fare is two cents more than one half of one penny more than it would be if fares had risen 50 percent this morning."

Now it was the passenger's turn to cogitate. What fare was he being asked for?

June 28

Let's revive a game from the 1940's known as "epithets" or "hinky-pinkies." For example, if we give you a brief phrase, such as "ill-natured taxi-driver," you have to translate it into a rhyming adjective-and-noun combination, such as "crabby cabby." Do you get the idea? One more example, and then you are on your own. Example: "Dracula and Frankenstein's monster." Your answer, hopefully, would be "gruesome twosome."

a. ardent employee
b. unimaginative surface decoration
c. a cactus that goes out of its way to upset you
d. a world of igneous rock
e. boisterous policy meeting
f. dismal chorus

June 29

Take the one-syllable word SMILE and insert an I into it. The result is SIMILE, a three-syllable word. By adding one letter, you have added two syllables. There are many transformations of this kind in English, and the letter added does not have to be on the inside. It can be added at the front (as in the case of VEAL-UVEAL) or at the back (as in the case of ROME-ROMEO). Following are six pairs of definitions, the length of each defined word being shown in brackets. The shorter word of each pair is one syllable long, and the longer word, differing only by a single letter, is three syllables long. Can you determine the dozen words?

a. visited (4)
   a gem with a figure carved in relief (5)

b. a day in the ancient Roman calendar (4)
   thoughts (5)

c. a legal violation (5)
   a Russian peninsula extending into Europe (6)

d. a legal right (4)
   foreign (5)

e. travelled on horseback (4)
   an exhibition of cowboy skills (5)

f. to utter a plaintive cry (5)
   a Maori woman (6)

June 30

On April 18 and April 26, we tested your knowledge of film titles, but how well do you know the actors and actresses who appear in films? If we were to give you this sequence of vowels and dashes: —AU——E——A—, would you be able to fill in the missing consonants and arrive at PAUL NEWMAN? Now try your hand at the following ones.

a. — A — — E — — EA — — Y
b. — O — E — — — E — — O — —
c. A — — A — I — O
d. E — — IO — — — OU — —
e. — A — — — A — — — EI — A — —
f. — EA — — O — — E — Y
g. — A — — E — — A — — — AU
h. — — E — — A — A — — — O —
i. — A — E — O — — A
j. — U — IE A — — — E — —

72

July 1

Below are clues for ten words. Against each clue is an indication of the word's length, and also where the letters JULY occur in the word. See if you can sort out what the complete words are. As an example, if the clue was "in a mirthful fashion" and the letter pattern was J———U—LY, you should be able to work out that the answer is JOYOUSLY.

JU — — L — — — — Y	rejoicingly
JU — — — — — L — Y	impartially
JU — — L — — Y	trickery
JU — — LY	accurately
JU — — — — L — — Y	childish character
— — JU — — — LY	joinedly
J — — U — — LY	in an arid manner
J — U — — — LY	swaggeringly
— — JU — — — — — — LY	in an ill-judged manner
— — — JU — — L — Y	marriage

July 2

On various days in this book, you will have come across word squares. Now examine, if you will, the following two word squares:

```
F I R S T
I R A T E        R A T
R A C E R        A C E
S T E A M        T E A
T E R M S
```

Note that the three-by-three square on the right is at the center of the five-by-five square on the left. There aren't many five-by-five squares where the middle nine letters themselves form a word square. Given the three-by-three square below, can you add 16 letters around its edges so as to turn it into a proper five-by-five word square?

W A R
A D A
R A T

July 3

Young Euclid was given a certain number to multiply by 409, but he made a blunder that is very common with children when learning the elements of simple arithmetic. He placed the first figure of his product by 4 below the second figure from the right, instead of below the third. We have probably all done that as youngsters when there has happened to be a zero in the multiplier. The result of Euclid's mistake was that his answer was wrong by 328,320, entirely because of that little slip. Now, what was the number that Euclid had been asked to multiply by 409? This is rather a simple puzzle.

July 4

Independence Day

The Revolution and the War of Independence occupied the years 1763–1783, and the Declaration of Independence was made on July 4, 1776. We could ask you to find a particularly apt anagram of the phrase THE AMERICAN REVOLUTION, such as the two below, but we won't.

HA! OUR MEN INCITE A REVOLT!
UNITE TO REVILE A MONARCH!

Instead, we shall ask you to devise an anagram of the phrase THE DECLARATION OF INDEPENDENCE. You might come up with something like DEFIAL PENNED A CONCEITED THRONE or

A FREE CLAN THEN DECIDED ONE POINT, but we are sure that you can do better than these.

July 5

Statistics indicate that men drivers are involved in more accidents than women drivers. It may be concluded that:

a. As usual, male chauvinists are wrong about women's abilities.
b. Men are actually better drivers but drive more frequently.
c. Men and women drive equally well but men cover more miles.
d. Most truck drivers are men.
e. Sufficient information is not available to justify a conclusion.

Which is it?

July 6

Each of five bars in the same town has a highly proficient darts team. In a series of matches organized last year, each bar's team played a match against each of the other four teams. The matches took place on five successive Saturdays: two matches each Saturday while one team had a bye. On the first Saturday, the Dew Drop Inn played the Atlantic Cafe. On the second Saturday, the Blue Balloon played McSurley's; the Blue Balloon, who won this match, triumphed the following week against Jimmy's Tavern. On the fourth Saturday, McSurley's had the bye. Who had the bye on the fifth Saturday?

July 7

A certain family party consisted of 1 grandfather, 1 grandmother, 2 fathers, 2 mothers, 4 children, 3 grandchildren, 1 brother, 2 sisters, 2 sons, 2 daughters, 1 father-in-law, 1 mother-in-law, and 1 daughter-in-law. A total of 23 people, you might think. But, no; there were only 7 people present. Can you show how this might be?

July 8

If OLLIE amounts to 31,770, and ELSIE is worth just 197 less, what value should you place on LESLIE?

July 9

Here is another word square puzzle, this one using six different six-letter words. Just solve the six clues given below. The answers, taken in order, will form the word square.

a. obliterates
b. ruler
c. program
d. transmitter
e. to make dear
f. like certain heavenly bodies

July 10

On January 7, we dabbled with various letter patterns displayed by five-letter words. For example, we saw that POKER, with no repeated letters, had the pattern 12345; we saw that TRUTH, with the first and fourth letters repeated, had the pattern 12314; we saw that CYNIC, with the first and fifth letters repeated, had the pattern 12341; and we saw that MADAM, with the first and fifth letters repeated, as well as the second and fourth ones, had the pattern 12321. Of course, the same sort of exercise can be undertaken with six-letter words. So, the following six-letter words have the patterns shown:

SENSES — 123121	TITBIT — 121321
HUBBUB — 123323	MAMMAL — 121123
SETTEE — 123322	ACACIA — 121231

Now, perhaps you would care to search for a dozen common words displaying the patterns below.

123232	122323	121133	123123
123321	122131	122321	123212
122132	121223	123443	123344

July 11

The beginning of eternity,
The end of time and space,
The beginning of every end,
The end of every place.

What can be described in this way?

July 12

Two ferries start at the same time from opposite sides of a river, traveling across the water on routes at right angles to the shores. Each boat travels at a constant speed, though their two speeds are different. They pass at a point 720 yards from the nearer shore. Both boats remain at their slips for ten minutes before starting back. On the return trips, they meet 400 yards from the other shore. How wide is the river?

July 13

When visiting a prison, I asked two of the inmates to give me their ages. They did so, and then, to test their arithmetical powers, I asked each of them to add the two ages together. One gave me 44 as the answer, and the other gave me 1280. I immediately saw that one of them had subtracted one age from the other, while the other inmate had multiplied the two ages together. Can you tell what the inmates' ages were?

July 14

Bastille Day

The storming of the Bastille (July 14, 1789) was the event that marked the beginning of the French Revolution. The Paris mob regarded the fortress-prison as the symbol of despotic rule. The anniversay of its capture is still kept as a national holiday commemorating the Revolution.

Using only the letters in BASTILLE, can you delete one letter, and rearrange the remaining letters to form a seven-letter word? Can you repeat this three times, ending up with three other different seven-letter words?

Using only letters which are in BASTILLE, make four six-letter words, all using the B and not including any plurals. Now make eight five-letter words from the letters in BASTILLE, all of them using the B, and no plurals. And finally, make ten four-letter words, all using the B, and, again, no plurals.

July 15

I am a word of 11 letters.
My 4, 9, 5 is worn on the head.
My 10, 9, 1, 11 is a narrow road.
My 11, 2, 3, 4, 5 is a number.
My 8, 6, 7 is a spirit.
My whole is an excellent songster.

What am I?

July 16

A man had a clock with an hour hand and a minute hand of the same length and indistinguishable. If the clock was set going at noon, what would be the first time that it would be impossible, by reason of the similarity of the hands, to be sure of the correct time? In grappling with this little problem, you may assume that it is possible to indicate fractions of a second. On this assumption, an exact answer can be given.

July 17

Back in the year 1936, poeple born in 1892 were able to make an unusual mathematical boast, a boast that people born in 1980 will be able to make at some time during the 21st century. John Stuart Mill, the English philosopher and economist, would also have been able to make the same boast, had he noticed it. Given that he was born in the 19th century, can you tell us which year?

July 18

My first is a number, my second another,
And each, I assure you, will rhyme with the other.
My first you will find is one-fifth of my second,
And truly my whole a long period reckoned.
Yet my first and my second (nay, think not I cozen),
When added together will make but two dozen.

How many am I?

July 19

When three quite ordinary words are "telescoped" together, like those given here, it is not always easy to recognize them, even though their letters are in the correct order. For example, given NONCABLEROPE, would you be able to spot that it was made up from ABLE, CROP and NONE? Now try the eight given here, bearing in mind that each is made up from three four-letter words.

AUTUMNSKILTS
SPRINGELATES
SUMMERCARPET
WINTERSTINTS
BEARORPUZZLE
TRANSPENDING
JOSEPHINEINE
OMARVLAMBERT

July 20

What statement is represented by the following?

STAND	TAKE	MINE	TAKING
I	U	2	MY

July 21

On February 18, we saw that the numbers 1 to 9 can be arranged in the form of a square, as shown below, so that each row of numbers has a common total, each column of numbers has the same common total, and the numbers in each of the two diagonals have the same total. We called this a "magic square."

$$8\ 1\ 6$$
$$3\ 5\ 7$$
$$4\ 9\ 2$$

Now, can you arrange the numbers 1 to 25 so as to form a magic square? This square will have five numbers in each row, column, and diagonal. And the numbers in each of these will add up to the same total.

July 22

Each of the items displayed here represents a familiar word, name, phrase or saying. For example, CCCCCCC can be recognized immediately as The Seven Seas. Now have fun with these!

a. JOANB

b. atte

c. cTo be or not to be c

d. aBADge

e. GENT

> c (above GENT)
> a (below GENT)

f. i.e..

g. theTHE

h. OP C STANT LE

July 23

Yesterday, you tackled eight familiar words, names and phrases which we had disguised. Now try eight more!

a. '8'

b. $_3$NT,$_4$H,$_5$C,6D

c. revilO

d. eveningAM

e. trohsLEFTright

f. b — — — — — e — — — — — d

g. carknaveton

h. atmosomethingsphere

July 24

If we multiply 64253 by 365, we get the product 23452345, where the first four figures are repeated. What is the largest number that can be multiplied by 365 to produce a similar product of eight figures with the first four figures repeated in the same order? There is no objection to a repetition of figures—that is, the four that are repeated need not all be different, as in the case shown here.

July 25

Of the three finalists in the bathing-beauty contest, Susan is older than the redhead, but younger than the hairdresser. Bernice is younger than the blonde, while Caroline is older than the brunette. The typist is the receptionist's younger sister. Can you give the haircoloring and profession of each girl in order of age?

July 26

The sentence below is George Bernard Shaw's comment on chess. Can you reconstruct the original quotation?

they clever are time making expedient foolish doing wasting very something for idle is a they chess people when their are only believe

July 27

Two railway trains, one 400 feet long and the other 200 feet long, ran on parallel tracks. It was found that when they went in opposite directions, they passed each other in five seconds, but when they ran in the same direction, the faster train would pass the other in fifteeen seconds. A curious passenger worked out the speed of each train from these facts. This, of course, assumes that both trains run at constant speeds. Can you work out the trains' speeds?

July 28

A traveler in the desert, meeting three nomads about to consume some camel's milk, asks whether they would share it with him for a price. They agree and pool the milk, the first contributing one pint more than the second, and the second contributing one pint more than the third. They share the milk equally. On leaving, the traveler gives them a sum of money. After some calculation, they decide that the first nomad should equitably get twice as much money as the second nomad. How much should the third nomad get?

July 29

These ten fictitious names are all rearrangements of the names of famous people. For example, if Sheila O'Norton was in the list, you would discover that this was really Horatio Nelson in disguise. Can you discover who everyone really is?

a. Jamie Braser   f. Jon Hasket
b. Frank Cardise   g. Fred Hyron
c. Fred Colatis   h. Mark Larx
d. Alfie Dondee   i. Helmut Tarrin
e. Fidel Haltor   j. June Seatan

July 30

A set of dominoes usually consists of 28 rectangular tiles. Each tile has two squares, each numbered from 0 to 6. Every combination of two numbers is represented. The basic rule in playing dominoes, of course, is that, in adding to a chain, you have to match the value of one square of your tile to the value of a square at one end of the chain. If you place all 28 dominoes in a continuous chain, bearing in mind that adjacent ends of tiles must match, so that 5 dots are at one end, how many will be at the other end of the chain? Try solving this mentally before checking with an actual set of dominoes.

July 31

Insert in the blank space between each of the two matched syllables below a syllable that will make one word out of the first syllable, and another out of the second.

a. BACK — ROBE   f. DOOR — STONE
b. BAR — DER   g. EX — TIVE
c. BOR — IVE   h. FIRE — WAYS
d. COM — EY   i. FOOT — SON
e. CUR — TED   j. FRET — MILL

August 1

It is often possible to take a word and remove each of its letters in succession, each time rearranging the letters left to form another word. For example, the word ANGRIEST can be operated on in such a way to produce the following words:

ANGRIEST - A = stinger
ANGRIEST - N = stagier
ANGRIEST - G = nastier
ANGRIEST - R = teasing
ANGRIEST - I = garnets
ANGRIEST - E = ratings
ANGRIEST - S = tearing
ANGRIEST - T = gainers

What we now want you to do is repeat this exercise, using a competely different set of words to the ones used above.

84

August 2

Below are clues for ten words. Against each clue is an indication of the word's length, and also where the letters AUG occur in the word. See if you can sort out what the complete words are. As an example, if the clue was "to make larger" and the letter pattern was AUG————, you should be able to work out that the answer is AUGMENT.

AUG ——————	a saint
— AUG — —	trapped
— — AUG —————	to induct formally into an office
— AUG ————	a female relative
— AUG —————	ludicrous
A — — U — — — G	bringing a charge against
— A — — — U ———— G	shooting out from
— AU — — G —	something to eat
A — — U — — G —	to diminish
— AUG ————————	arrogance

August 3

There are several letters which are well known to occur doubled in many words. Double L, double T, and double S are all pretty common. But can you find words containing the following doubled letters? Your answers might be very obscure, but they need not be. Our answers are all perfectly common words in everyday use.

HH   II   KK   UU   VV   WW

August 4

Here are the names of a dozen countries and regions, all in scrambled form. How many of them can you recognize?

a. chain	g. rumba
b. enemy	h. unsad
c. erect	i. analog
d. laity	j. serial
e. plane	k. sprucy
f. reign	l. regalia

August 5

A man left a legacy of $10,000 to three relatives and their wives. Together, the wives received $3960. June received $100 more than Camille, and Martha received $100 more than June. Jack Smith was given just as much as his wife, Horace Saunders got half as much again as his wife, and Terry Conners received twice as much as his wife. What was the first name of each man's wife?

August 6

```
T H I S
    I S
V E R Y
─────────
E A S Y
```

This is really an addition problem incognito. You must replace each letter by one of the digits. The same digit must be used to represent the same letter. Put in the numbers for the letters and get a perfectly valid addition problem.

August 7

So far in this book, all the word squares which we have met have had the same down words as across words. Word squares don't necessarily have to possess this property. It is possible to devise word squares where *all* the words used are different, with none of the down words being the same as the across words. Here is an example:

S P A C E

L E M O N

I N E P T

M A N S E

E L D E R

Given below are ten clues, five for the across words and five for the down words. See if you can solve the clues and arrive at the required word square.

Across clues: a fruit; to rest; to harangue; a person who works in a mine; characterized by briskness

Down clues: delicate smell; a danger; a flat area; after; to do by effort

August 8

Smith and Jones each secretly write down a number between 1 and 100. The object of the game is to guess the other player's number first. Questions may be asked concerning the opponent's number provided that they can be answered truthfully by a YES or a NO. A player is allowed to continue asking questions so long as he receives YES answers. The first NO answer transfers the role of questioner to the opponent. The conservative "Twenty Questions" strategy of questioning in such a manner as to most nearly equalize the chances of YES and NO answers is most effective in that particular game. Using it, you can, in only 20 questions, invariably pinpoint any number in the range of 1 to 500,000. But in the game outlined above, this may not be the best way to proceed. Suppose you are the first player. What will your questioning strategy be, and how much of an advantage do you feel you have over your opponent?

August 9

Booklets designed to acquaint small children with the alphabet usually contain entries such as "A is for Apple, B is for Ball, C is for Cat . . . . . Z is for Zoo." Apart from the obvious unimaginativeness of this fare, it is misleading, for ordinary words use silent letters. It would be more realistic and more instructive to teach children an alphabet such as "A is for Hoarse, B is for Lamb, C is for Czar, ... Z is for Pince-nez."

What we now want you to do is fill in the 22 missing letters in our new alphabet. Find words in which the 22 letters from D to Y are silent. We have shown you the way. Can you finish the job?

August 10

Two grandmothers, with their two granddaughters;
Two husbands, with their two wives;
Two fathers, with their two daughters;
Two mothers, with their two sons;
Two maidens, with their two mothers;
Two sisters, with their two brothers;
Yet only six in all lie buried here;
All born legitimate, from incest clear.

This 16th century epitaph can be explained. How is everyone related?

August 11

Testing and teasing his father's memory, a boy asked his father, "How many kings have been crowned in England since the Conquest?"

"Son," replied his dad, "I have not been to school as recently as you. I used to know all the kings and queens by heart, and the dates of their coronations, but I doubt if I can remember them all now.''

"There's no need to waste your time with such a list," was the reply, "for there was only one." Who was it?

August 12

Start off with the word GROUSE. Delete one letter and rearrange the remaining letters to make a word. Now delete one letter from this new word and rearrange the letters to make yet another new word. Keep doing this until there is only one letter left. Now repeat the exercise, but using different words. Now repeat the exercise again, still using different words!

August 13

Anniversary of Florence Nightingale's death (1910)

Take the letters in the name of FLORENCE NIGHTINGALE and rearrange them so as to make a particularly apt phrase or saying which could be applied to her. Remember, it must be of some relevance to Florence Nightingale or nursing.

August 14

Boris, Sergei, Tam and Viktor are weight-lifters. Viktor can outlift Tam, but Sergei can outlift Viktor. Tam can outlift Boris, but Sergei can outlift Tam. Therefore:

a. Both Boris and Sergei can outlift Viktor
b. Viktor can outlift Boris but can't outlift Tam
c. Viktor can outlift Boris by more than he can outlift Tam
d. None of the above

Which of these is correct?

August 15

Two days ago, we asked you to find an apt anagram of Florence Nightingale's name. We could do the same for SIR WALTER SCOTT. But you would probably think that LAST SCOT WRITER was too easy to find. So, instead, we've made the problem slightly harder. Try and devise an apt anagram for the following phrase:

IVANHOE, BY SIR WALTER SCOTT

You don't need to retain the comma, just the letters. We will be interested to see what you can come up with.

August 16

One-third of an hour after a candle was lit, the other end was also lit. It took a further one-third of an hour for the candle to burn out. If the candle was lit at both ends at the start, and one end was quenched when only the middle one-third of the candle remained, how long in all would it take to burn the candle out?

August 17

With thieves I consort,
With the vilest, in short,
I'm quite at my ease in depravity;
Yet all divines use me,
And savants can't lose me,
For I am the center of gravity.

Who or what am I?

August 18

Earlier this year, on May 6 and June 6, we presented the titles of various novels, but with all the consonants replaced by blanks. Your task was to identify the novels. As an example, we gave ——EI——I—I——E—A—, which turns out to be THE IN-VISIBLE MAN. Here are ten more novels for you to get to grips with. See how well you do.

a. ——E—I——I———E—I——O——
b. —I——IE——E—OO—
c. —O—E—I——O—E
d. —U——E—I———EI————
e. —E———A———O
f. —O——O—E—
g. —O—O—U——AY
h. ——E——O——OO—E
i. —I———A—,—OO——A—
j. —I——I—I——I—A—I

August 19

If two boys and a girl can beat their father in a tug-of-war, but their mother can win against a boy and two girls, who should win a contest between the father and a girl against the mother and a boy?

August 20

Three cars had driven into a parking lot at the same time, and the three drivers left them all for the attendant to park. Unfortunately, he isn't too good at remembering exactly which driver drove which car. However, he is sure of these six facts:

a. Colin drove the BMW if and only if Mr. Cooper drove the Avenger
b. Alan drove the Cortina if and only if Mr. Cooper drove the BMW
c. Colin is Mr. Brown if and only if Mr. Andrews drove the BMW
d. Brian is Mr. Andrews if and only if Colin drove the BMW
e. Mr. Cooper drove the Avenger if and only if Alan is Mr. Brown
f. Colin is Mr. Brown if and only if Alan drove the Cortina

How long will it take you to deduce the first and last names for each car's driver?

August 21

Dictionaries abound with terms like EMPEROR PENGUIN, FALLOW DEER, FLYING FOX and POLAR BEAR, all obviously the names of animals. Given below are two lists of ten words. The first is a list of apparently random words, and the second is a list of animals. Can you pair off the words in the lists so as to make ten dictionary-recognized terms? For example, if POLAR was in the first list and BEAR in the second, you would pair them off to make POLAR BEAR. Once you have paired off all the words, see if you notice anything peculiar about the ten terms.

desert	black	Bull	vulture
lame	Cheshire	cat	fish
eager	Welsh	rabbit	beaver
queer	dark	sheep	rat
John	culture	horse	duck

August 22

Mr. Grumper grumbles about bad time-keeping on the trains like everybody else. On one particular morning he was justified, though. The train left on time for the one-hour journey and it arrived 5 minutes late. However, Mr. Grumper's watch showed it to be 3 minutes early, so he adjusted his watch by putting it forward 3 minutes. His watch kept time during the day, and on the return journey in the evening the train started on time, according to his watch, and arrived on time, according to the station clock. If the train traveled 25 percent faster on the return journey than it did on the morning journey, was the station clock fast or slow, and by how much?

August 23

Certain words have other complete words contained within them. For example, BEVERAGE has EVER embedded in it. Given here are ten pairs of definitions, the first defintion of each pair referring to the included word, and the second definition referring to the longer word. How long will it take you to discover them all?

a. source & native inhabitants
b. corrosion & thwarted
c. reliable & not hastily
d. neat & marriage
e. health resort & media
f. uproar & country lovers
g. vindicate & cleanser
h. ring and revolt
i. stupid person & clergyman's robe
j. make certain & blame

August 24

$$AB + CD + (EF/GH) + (I/J) = 100$$

Each of the ten digits from 0 to 9 has been used once and only once in the construction of the above sum. Can you replace the letters with the digits? There is more than one valid answer, so when you have found one answer, see if you can find others.

August 25

Arrange the ten digits 0 to 9 in three arithmetical sums, using three of the four operations of addition, subtraction, multiplication and division, and using no signs except the ordinary ones implying those operations. Here is an example to make it quite clear:

$$3 + 4 = 7 \qquad 9 - 8 = 1 \qquad 5 \times 6 = 30$$

But this is not correct, as 2 has been omitted and 3 has been used twice. Now it's your turn.

August 26

Can you find common English words containing the following groups of three letters consecutively? For example, MMU exists in AMMUNITION, but we are sure you will be able to find an alternative to that.

BBT	CCR	DDM	FFH
GGH	HHO	KKN	LLJ
MMU	NNK	PPH	RRH
SSP	TTH	VVY	WWO

August 27

This is another of our large collection of clock puzzles, where clocks do strange and wonderful things. I dreamed that I was traveling in a strange country. Most of the details of the dream are lost to me, but I do remember one particular incident. I had seen a clock, announced the time as it appeared to be shown, but my guide had then corrected me. He said, "You are unaware that the minute hand always moves in the opposite direction to the hour hand. Except for this improvement, our clocks are precisely the same as those you are used to."

Since the hands were exactly together between the hours of four and five o'clock, and they started together at noon, what was the real time?

August 28

Can you arrange the odd digits 1, 3, 5, 7 and 9, and the even digits, 2, 4, 6 and 8, in such a way that the odd ones add up to the same as the even ones? You can use arithmetical signs and decimals, but the idea is to try and arrive at the simplest possible solution. There are, as you might imagine, innumerable answers of increasing perplexity.

August 29

In each of the following sentences is hidden the name of a country. For example, in the sentence "His painstaking efforts were much admired," SPAIN is hidden in the first two words.

a. Couples wed entirely of their own accord nowadays.
b. There isn't a catch in any of these questions.
c. The newly-elected sheriff ran celebrities out of town.
d. Her bank withdrawal established a new all-time record.
e. Struggling against the strong wind, I advanced very slowly.
f. They easily scan a day's order forms in the morning.

August 30

Imagine some people seated around a table playing the following game for the first time. Cyclically and in turn, starting with a player selected at random, they must name a land mammal starting with successive letters of the alphabet. Thus the game might begin with the first player saying APE, the second player saying BISON, the third player saying CAMEL, and so on. The time limit on each turn is 10 seconds. Without playing the game mentally, you are asked to predict the first letter on which a player will draw a complete blank.

August 31

This is an unusual day, and so is this paragraph. How quickly can you find out what is so uncommon about it? It looks so ordinary that you may think nothing is odd about it until you match it with most paragraphs this long. If you put your mind to it, and study it, you will find out, but nobody may assist you. Do it without any coaching. Go to work and try your skill at figuring it out. Par on it is about half an hour. Good luck!

September 1

On August 7, we saw that the down and across words in a word square don't necessarily have to be the same, and this square was given as an example:

```
S P A C E
L E M O N
I N E P T
M A N S E
E L D E R
```

Given below are ten clues, five for the across words and five for the down words. See if you can solve the clues and arrive at the required word square.

Across words: a crime; a friendly salutation; a device for communication; not concealed; to moor

Down words: to vibrate; to shove; a person who occupies the office of judge or ruler; to trifle; a projection on a saw or wheel

September 2

Below are clues for a dozen words. Against each clue is an indication of the word's length, and also where the letters SEP, TEM or BER occur in the word. See if you can sort out what the complete words are. As an example, if the clue was "one who tends sheep" and the letter pattern was S — EP — — — —, you should be able to work out that the answer is SHEPHERD.

S — — EP — — — — — —	one who repairs chimneys
T — E — M — — — — — —	a device for measuring temperature
— — B — ER — — — —	an evasive ploy
SEP — — — — — —	a tomb
TEM — — — —	a violent wind storm
BER — — — — — —	a chemical element
— — — — SEP —	part of a church
— — — TEM — —	scorn
— — — BER	quantity
S — E — P —	drowsy
— T — E — M	a river
B — E — R —	watery

September 3

On several occasions, we have seen that the letters CCCCCCC can be interpreted as The Seven Seas. Now see if you can make sense of the seven given here.

   a. sopBACTRIAN   b. milonelion

c. Sympho

d. IME

e. $\begin{smallmatrix}L\\G\end{smallmatrix}$Man

f. $\begin{smallmatrix}L\\EMOC\end{smallmatrix}$2me

g. gunGUNgun
   GUNgunGUN

September 4

Long ago when gas was 46 cents a gallon, I once pulled into a garage in my truck to fill up my tank. I proffered a $20 bill to the attendant, and waited to receive my change. Unfortunately, the attendant charged me the number of dollars that I had bought gallons—for example, if I had bought 5.7 gallons, he would have charged me $5.70. As a result of this, I received less change than I should have. Though this was immediately obvious to me, the remarkable thing was that I had received in change exactly the amount that I should have been charged for gas in the first place. Remembering that the cash indicator on a gas pump will only charge to the nearest half-cent, how many gallons of gas did I buy that day?

September 5

By adding a C to each of the words below, then shuffling the letters, it is possible to form a new work. Add another C, shuffle again, and a third word appears. For example, by adding C to ESAU, you can create CAUSE. Add another C, and you have ACCUSE. Get the idea? See how many you can solve—steer clear of plurals and verbs ending in S, though.

oil	tape	here	lean	lout
hat	oust	near	hate	spite
ark	oast	sear	head	nose
irk	rose	sour	rile	neat

September 6

What is the lowest number which requires the five vowels A, E, I, O and U once each in its spelling? What is the lowest number which requires the six vowels A, E, I, O, U and Y once each in its spelling?

September 7

The square of 13 is 169. Take the last digit of the square, 9, and place it in the middle, making 196. This is the square of 14, the next number above 13. What are the next numbers which also have this property?

September 8

Some 794 letters make up the words for the numbers from one through to ninety-nine. Among them all, I notice, there are only two L's. In an effort to determine the significance of this blatant alphabetical discrimination, I checked the frequency of the other letters in the same set of words. How many A's are there? None! How many B's? None! How many C's? None! How many D's? None! Clearly, simple arithmetic seems to be a select club which arbitrarily excludes some of the finest letters of the alphabet! And where, too, are J, K, M, P, Q and Z? Nowhere! I wonder if you can say which two numbers contain the L's — ten seconds is your time limit.

September 9

The black and white minstrels decided to do a red, white and blue jubilee routine. As you probably know, there are 48 minstrels. 16 of them have red hair, 16 have dark hair, and 16 have fair hair.

In their jubilee routine, 16 wear red costumes, 16 wear white costumes, and 16 wear blue costumes. At dress rehearsal, someone noticed that three of the white-costumed minstrels had red hair, and five of the red-costumed dancers had fair hair. Furthermore, no two hair color/costume color groups had the same number of dancers. So, how many of the dark-haired minstrels wore blue costumes in the jubilee routine?

September 10

The kung fu club had been meeting in the same building for a couple of years on a no-charge basis. Then the owner announced that the members would have to pay or stop using the building. It was agreed in the club that two representatives should go and talk to the owner. There was no trouble selecting a group of three men from whom the two would be chosen. But the final two were selected only after some trouble. Each of the three was named by one of the others as an unacceptable team mate. Which two men finally went to see the owner? First and last names, and occupations, please.

a. Dan refused to go with Mr. Brady
b. Mr. Paine refused to go with the chemist
c. Jim refused to go with the salesman
d. Peter is not Mr. Paine
e. Mr. Hall is not the salesman
f. The artist is not Jim

September 11

My friend Richard, who lives in the country, caught an earlier train home than usual yesterday. His wife normally drives the family car to the station to meet him. But yesterday, he set out on foot from the station to meet his wife part way in the car. He reached home 12 minutes earlier than he would have done had he waited at the station for his wife. The car can travel at a uniform speed which is five times Richard's speed on foot. Richard arrived home just as the clock was correctly striking six o'clock. At what time would he have reached home if his wife, forewarned of his change of plan, had met him at the station?

September 12

RAP is an interesting word, because it is possible to create new words by adding a letter in front of the R, between the R and A, between the A and P, and after the P. Thus, TRAP, REAP, RASP, and RAPT. Can you find a four-letter word similar to RAP? And a five-letter word?

September 13

Take the word ORIENTALS. Delete one letter and rearrange the remaining letters to make another word. Now delete one letter from this new word and rearrange the remaining letters to make another new word. Keep doing this until there is only one letter left.

September 14

If you were given this arrangement of letters:

$$- - TR - - CH$$

you ought to be able to fill both pairs of blank spaces with the same letters so as to make a word. In this particular case, you should insert EN into each pair of blank spaces, making the word ENTRENCH. Given the following arrangements of letters, can you work out which letters need to be added to make words in the same fashion?

a. $--$ID$--$LE	f. $--$IL$--$SY
b. $--$RM$--$LS	g. $--$MI$--$ZE
c. $--$RE$--$CK	h. $--$VE$--$RN
d. $--$UR$--$ES	i. $--$ST$--$NE
e. $--$CA$--$NT	j. $--$MA$--$ES

September 15

In this little multiplication sum the five letters represent five different digits. What are the actual figures? There are no zeros involved.

$$
\begin{array}{r}
S\ E\ A\ M \\
T \\
\hline
M\ E\ A\ T\ S
\end{array}
$$

September 16

A mixed packet of nuts contains 1 pound of walnuts and 2 pounds of Brazil nuts. It costs exactly $2. A packet containing 4 pounds of filberts and 1 pound of walnuts costs $3. And for only $1.50, you can buy a mixed packet of 3 pounds of almonds, 1 pound of walnuts, and 1 pound of filberts. How much should you pay for a mixture of 1 pound of each of the four kinds?

September 17

Three men were arguing as to which of them was the wealthiest. Three different measurements of wealth were invoked, and none of the men came first and last in any two of them. Mr. Edwards spends less per year than Claudette's husband, but has more capital than Graham. Benjamin has more capital than Mr. Hayes.

Mr. Edwards spends less per year than Claudette's husband. Benjamin spends more per year than Iris' husband and also has more capital, but his annual income is less than Mr. Daventry's. Is Annabelle married to Felix? And who has the smallest annual income?

September 18

Samuel Johnson's birthday (1709)

Dictionaries define JOHNSONESE in the following manner: "ponderous English, full of antitheses and words of classical origin." The word is derived from the name of Dr. Samuel Johnson, the British lexicographer, who lived between 1709 and 1784. Johnson dominated the lexicographic world of the 18th century with his monumental dictionary which was published in 1755. Johnson had a great love of ornate diction and his pride in his mastery of it allowed him to contrive definitions for some of his words in his dictionary that were so intricate as to arouse amusement even in his own day. Given below are definitions of three common English words taken from Johnson's dictionary. The definitions highlight what is meant by the term JOHNSONESE. See if you can decide which three words Johnson was defining.

a. an exotic and irrational entertainment
b. a convulsion of the lungs, vellicated by some sharp serosity
c. anything reticulated or decussated at equal distances, with interstices between the intersections

September 19

ABSTEMIOUS and FACETIOUS are two words which contain the five vowels in order. There are plenty of other words which contain just one occurrence of each of the five vowels, though not in order. ANXIOUSNESS contains the vowels in the order AIOUE, ENCOURAGING has them in the order EOUAI, and

INOCULATE has them in the order IOUAE. See if you can find words which contain the five vowels in the orders shown below.

AIEOU	IOUAE
AOUIE	OAUIE
EAIOU	OUEAI
EUOIA	UAIOE
IAOUE	UOIAE

September 20

What common chemical compound is represented by the following letters: HIJKLMNO?

What number gives the same result when it is added to $1\frac{1}{2}$ and when it is multiplied by $1\frac{1}{2}$?

How many S's are there in the name of the longest river in the world?

What everyday English word is most often pronounced incorrectly?

What are the next two letters in this series:

    A   E   F   H   I   K   L   M?

September 21

My head and tail both equal are,
My middle slender as a bee.
Whether I stand on head or heel
Is quite the same to you or me.
But if my head should be cut off,
The matter's true, though passing strange
Directly I to nothing change.

What am I?

104

September 22

If a crab and a half weigh a pound and a half, but the half crab weighs half as much again as the whole crab, what do half the whole crab and the whole of the half crab weigh?

September 23

Two years ago, a man was offered a motorcycle for $1024, but he declined to buy it. A year later, he was offered the same motorcycle for $640, but again decided not to buy it. A little while after that, he was again offered the motorcycle, this time at $400. Again, he refused to buy it. Last week, he turned the motorcycle down even though the price had now fallen to $250. If the owner offers it for sale yet again, and he makes a consistent reduction, how much will it be for sale for the next time?

September 24

A chessboard has squares that are two inches by two inches. What is the diameter of the largest circle that can be drawn on the board in such a way that the circle's circumference is entirely on black squares?

September 25

On August 7 and September 1, we saw that the down and across words in a word square don't necessarily have to be the same, and this square was given as an example:

```
S P A C E
L E M O N
I  N E P T
M A N S E
E L D E R
```

Given below are ten clues, five for the across words and five for
the down words. See if you can solve the clues and arrive at the
required word square.

Across words: boggy ground; angry; to prise; to work flour into
    dough; jerks

Down words: lactic; a sphere of action, a bird; meat; groups of
    animals

September 26

T. S. Eliot's birthday (1888)

Hands up all those who knew that the T S in T. S. Eliot stood for
Thomas Stearns. Take the name THOMAS, delete one letter and
shuffle the remaining letters to form a new word. Delete a letter
from the new word, shuffle the remaining letters, and end up
with another new word. Continue doing this until just one letter
is left. Now repeat this little exercise with the name STEARNS.
And now repeat it with ELIOT.

September 27

The word ABSCOND has the four consecutive letters ABCD occurring in it and in that order. Indeed, the past tense ABSCONDED
contains the letters ABCDE. See if you can find words, like
ABSCOND, that possess the following groups of letters.

DEFG
FGHI

106

HIJK
MNOP
QRST
RSTU

September 28

What are the next two numbers in this series:

   1   4   13   28   49?

Which are there more of: inches in a mile or Sundays in a 1000 years?

Which are there more of: seconds in a week or feet in 100 miles?

Which are there more of: square feet in half a square mile or cubic yards in a cubic furlong?

Which number gives the same result when it is added to $3\frac{3}{4}$ as when it is multiplied by $3\frac{3}{4}$?

September 29

Seven clues are given below, each referring to a seven-letter word. The seven answers can be fitted into a 7-by-7 grid so as to complete a word square. Obviously, as there are only seven clues, there will only be seven different words in the square, the down words being the same as the across words.

combinations
immutable
a yacht race-meeting
attraction exerted by a body's presence
to give a right to
type of snake
killers

September 30

After collecting 770 shells, the three boys divided them up so that their amounts were in the same proportions as their ages. As often as Mike took four shells, Nick took three, and for every six that Mike received, Sam took seven. How many shells did each boy get?

October 1

Below are clues for ten words. Against each clue is an indication of the word's length, and also where the letters OCT occur in the word. See if you can sort out what the complete words are. As an example, if the clue was "a university official" and the letter pattern was — — OCT — —, you should be able to work out that the answer is PROCTOR.

OCT — — — — —	a large number
OC — — — T	a cat
— — — — OCT — — —	a preparation
O — C — — T	secret, esoteric
O — — — — CT	to exaggerate
— OC — — T	a missile
— O — C — — T — —	egotistical
OC — — — — T	a specialist in eye defects
— O — C — — T —	a mixture of sand, gravel and cement
OC — — — — — T	one who has possession

October 2

On several occasions, we have seen that the letters CCCCCCC can be interpreted as The Seven Seas. Now see if you can make sense of the eight clues given here:

a.
    I
    IIIIIII

b. DAYDAYOUT

c. entury

d. oholene

e. puritypiety

f. th th

g. N   NO NO NO
  R   NO NO NO
   YOUR
  U   NO NO NO
  T   NO NO NO

h. ttacks

October 3

New Orleans	3	St. Louis	3
Pittsburgh	2	Atlanta	3
Miami	3	Los Angeles	4
San Francisco	4	Seattle	3
Boston	2	Philadelphia	?

How many did Philadelphia score in their match with Boston?

October 4

What do all of these words have in common? Yes, they *are* all in the dictionary, but what *else* do they have in common?

gem	nave
yak	ailed
map	asset
lien	nomad

October 5

It's a common five-letter word that usually takes up a lot of space in any dictionary. A few of its definitions are given below. Can you identify the word?

Adjective: enveloping; with horizontal swing; plump; smooth and full-sounding; sonorous; well finished-off; periodic; approximate; full; plain-spoken; candid; honest; unsparing; vigorous; unqualified; without mincing

Adverb: about; on all sides; in a ring; in a curve; in rotation; indirectly; circuitously; in the neighborhood; towards the opposite quarter; every way

Preposition: about; around; on every side of; all over; past; beyond; to every side of in succession

Noun: a ladder rung; a slice of toast; a cut of beef; a brewer's vessel for beer; a coil; a bend; a circuit; a dance in a ring; a cycle; an accustomed walk; routine; a volley; a dealt portion; a bout in boxing

Verb: to surround; to finish off; to give a finish to make circular; to turn

October 6

A plane flies from Athens to Brussels at maximum speed. Normally, flying at maximum speed would enable it to reach Brussels in four-fifths of the time that it takes to fly there at cruising speed. On this occasion, however, the velocity of a favorable wind enables it to get there in only half the time it would normally take at maximum speed. On the return journey, it leaves Brussels at 1 p.m. Ignoring time zones, and encountering the same velocity and direction of wind, at what time will the plane arrive back at Athens?

October 7

Take the word STENTORIAN. Delete one letter and rearrange the remaining letters to make another word. Now delete one letter from this new word and rearrange the remaining letters to make another new word. Keep doing this until there is only one letter left.

October 8

Alison, Brenda and Carla usually have lunch together. When Alison was absent, the girl who walks to work went shopping with the secretary. When Brenda was off sick, the girl who lives with her sister had lunch with the girl who drives her own car to work. When Carla took a day off, the cashier and the girl who lives with her husband (her *own* husband!) both had to work through their lunch breaks. Recently, the girl who lives alone had an argument with the receptionist and with the girl who comes to work by bus. If the secretary drives herself to work, who lives with whom, what are their jobs, and how do they get to work?

October 9

How well do you know film titles? If we were to give you this sequence of vowels and dashes: $--E--I--$, would you be able to fill in the missing consonants and arrive at THE STING? Try your hand at the following ones, all the films are from the 1970's.

a. $---A--O--$
b. $-E-I-E-A--E$
c. $A--O---O--O-A--E$
d. $-O-E-I--I--E--O$
e. $-I--I----O--OY$
f. $-A---I--E$
g. $E-A-UE--E$
h. $--E-O--A--E-$
i. $-A---A--O\ I--A-I-$
j. $-I--Y-A--Y$

111

October 10

Here are definitions for ten words, all beginning with the letters TEN (such as TENANT, TENABLE, etc.). Can you say what the words are?

a. inclination   f. opinion held as true
b. delicate, gentle   g. racket game
c. a sinew   h. capable of being stretched
d. the wisp of a curl i. between bass and alto
e. dwelling place   j. stretched tight

October 11

Each of these three sentences contains three clues to the names of trees. Can you find all nine tree names?

a. The coastguard discovered the clear remains of a fire on the seashore.
b. "Don't just stand there and mope," urged my older brother. "Fight back!"
c. The couple are well-liked, but without doubt you will owe their friends a tidy sum.

October 12

Katie the cook was in a predicament over a pie. The recipe called for baking it for exactly nine continuous minutes, but all she had in the way of clocks were two egg-timers. The first one measured a period of four minutes, and the second one seven minutes. If there are no graduations on the egg-timers, and sand cannot be removed or transferred from them, what is the quickest way that Katie can measure nine minutes with the two timers?

October 13

The conversation in a bar returned frequently to age. The four men concerned considered their ages only in whole numbers of years. They found that:

a. Mr. Ashton is 10 years older than Brian
b. Mr. Cox is 10 years older than Charlie
c. Mr. Baldwin is 24 years old
d. David is the oldest of the four
e. The average age of the four is two years lower than the average age of Allen, Brian and David

The discussion took quite a while, during which:

f. Mr. Cox drank more beer than Brian
g. Charlie drank more beer than Mr. Denby
h. Allen drank more beer than David
i. Mr. Denby drank more beer than Mr. Ashton
j. Mr. Baldwin drank more beer than Mr. Cox

Describe all four men, giving their first and last names, their ages, and the relative amounts of beer consumed during the discussion.

October 14

In Cockney rhyming slang, the rhyming part is often omitted. For example, titfer (in full, tit for tat) is hat, and plates (plates of meat) are feet. Can you join each of the words in the first column to its rhyming part in the second column, find its meaning in the third column? For example, apples (from the first column) and pears (from the second column)—stairs (from the third column). Got the idea?

apples	and flute	beer
bees	and pears	boots
butcher's	and honey	garden
china	and strife	look
daisy	ear	mate
Dolly	hook	money
pig's	Lee	stairs
Rosie	plate	suit
trouble	roots	tea
whistle	Varden	wife

October 15

A shopkeeper packs his dog biscuits (all of the same quality) in boxes containing 16, 17, 23, 24, 39 and 40 pounds, and he is not prepared to sell them in any other way, nor break into a box. A customer asks to be supplied with exactly 100 pounds of biscuits. If you were the shopkeeper, could you meet the customer's requirement? If not, how near could you get to supplying the 100 pounds? You can assume, of course, that there is an ample supply of boxes of each size.

October 16

Oscar Wilde's birthday (1854)

Oscar Wilde's epigrams shocked and titillated late Victorian society. "I can resist everything," he said solemnly, "except temptation." Fox hunting he once described as "the unspeakable in full pursuit of the uneatable." Some other Wilde epigrams have been scrambled and are presented below. Put the words back in order if you can.

a. seriously to talk important is ever a far thing about life too

b. charming and good people are absurd, to divide either into tedious or bad people is it
c. us are we are in at but all some the stars of looking the gutter
d. the one play cards one winning has always fairly when should
e. in a sense romance spoils a woman as so much the humour of nothing
f. to be sure truth tells one later or if one is out the sooner found

October 17

Take a word like POT, add the letter U, and you have POUT. Described below are other pairs of words in which one becomes the other merely by the addition of a U. So, U can:

a. make avenging deities out of small fish
b. take a money holder and chase it
c. pry with a lever into an elevation
d. shade off into an academician
e. make a bird out of a letter
f. take a bony structure and make it lie flat
g. turn a news medium into a poor thing
h. go from satisfied to a fight
i. perform as a pair
j. change people into a list of food

October 18

Give us a common English word of 6 letters containing: (a) four E's; (b) four O's; (c) four S's.

Give us a common English word of 8 letters containing: (d) four F's; (e) four G's; (f) four R's.

There is only one genuinely English word ending with the two letters MT. What is it?

Can you think of a common English word beginning with: (g) a
double E; (h) a double L; (i) a double O?

There seems to be only one ordinary English word that can be
turned into another by replacing a U with a V. Find it.

October 19

There is a certain number whose third and fourth powers, taken
together, exhibit all the digits from 0 to 9, each once and once
only. Can you work out what the number is?

October 20

Curtail me thrice, I am a youth;
Behead me once, a snake;
Complete, I'm often used, in truth,
When certain steps you'd take.

Who or what am I?

October 21

Can you recognize words without their A's? Given here are a
dozen words from which exactly 39 A's have been extracted. See
if you can put back the missing A's. Each word has at least three
A's.

a. bnn   g. slm
b. prllx   h. mlyn
c. chrbnc   i. ctmrn
d. cnst   j. bccrt
e. dmnt   k. brcdbr
f. ngrm   l. mcdm

116

October 22

Which is the odd word out in this list, and why?

CONTRABAND   ROOK
HOURI   LEVITATE
ARCHAIC   EXPLOSION
YACHT   SUBMARINES

October 23

In the list of words below, a number of letters are missing from each word. These are indicated by the appropriate number of dashes. Each group of missing letters spells out a boy's name. Some of the names are in shortened forms, but all are well-known. Can you fathom out the names?

a. cla — — — le   f. a — — — ic
b. d — — — —   g. c — — — ice
c. — — — ba   h. gal — — — n
d. com — — — ible   i. pre — — — ent
e. l — — — l   j. cl — — — — al

October 24

This is just like yesterday's puzzle, except that each group of missing letters spells out a girl's name. Can you identify all the girls?

a. rea — — — e   f. b — — — — donna
b. arm — — —   g. tis — — —
c. s — — — nty   h. ma — — — — l
d. big — — —   i. pl — — — — r
e. sum — — — — — s   j. t — — — — ful

October 25

I have two coins whose sum is 55 cents. One of them is *not* a half dollar. What two coins do I have?

October 26

Three men went to a hotel and were told that there was only one room left and that it would cost $30 for the night. They paid $10 each and went to the room. The desk clerk subsequently realized that he had made a mistake and had overcharged the men $5. He asked one of the hotel's other staff to return the $5 to the men. This other employee was not as honest as the desk clerk, though. He reasoned that, since $5 is not easily divisible by 3, he would keep $2 and return $3 to the men, so that each would get back $1. Each man therefore only paid $9 each, which totals $27 for the room. Add to that the $2 that the hotel employee kept, and the total is only $29. What happened to the missing $1? Who had it, where did it go?

October 27

What, if anything, can be deduced from the following three statements?

a. No experienced person is incompetent
b. Mr. Jones is always blundering
c. No competent person is always blundering

October 28

Here are seven clues for seven seven-letter words. Solve the clues and write the answers, in order, one under the other. The resulting arrangement should be a word square with the across words the same as the down words.

a. declares strongly
b. bondage
c. liquids secreted in the mouth
d. obvious
e. to change round
f. a cross-beam
g. groups, or sets of things

October 29

Q W E R T Y U I O P
A S D F G H J K L
Z X C V B N M

This is the order in which letters appear on a standard typewriter keyboard. ASH, RUG and TUG are three words whose letters occur in "typewriter order." Can you find longer examples? What is the longest such word you can find? In searching for words, it may help to know that doubled letters (as in the word WOO) are acceptable.

October 30

Which gives the largest result: multiplying together all the numbers from 1 to 10 or all the even numbers from 1 to 16?

Which are there more of: millimeters in a mile or seconds in a month?

What is the value of one-half of two-thirds of three-quarters of four-fifths of five-sixths of six-sevenths of seven-eighths of eight-ninths of nine-tenths of 30?

Write down a mathematical expression, having a value of 24, which uses three equal digits, none of them being 8.

Write down three mathematical expressions, each having a value of 30, each of which uses three equal digits.

October 31

Y Y U R

Y Y U B

I C U R

Y Y 4 M E

The above piece of "verse" is probably familiar to most school-children. In plain English, it reads: "Too wise you are, too wise you be, I see you are too wise for me." Perhaps you would care to have a go at translating the following piece of dialogue between a customer and a waitress.

F U N E X ?

S V F X

F U N E M ?

S V F M

O K L F M N X

November 1

Below are clues for ten words. Against each clue is an indication of the word's length, and also where the letters NOV occur in the word. See if you can sort out what the complete words are. As an example, if the clue was "to expose" and the letter pattern was $-N-OV--$, you should be able to work out that the answer is UNCOVER.

NOV $----$	newness
$--$NOV $-----$	the introduction of something new
$--$N$--$OV$----$	contention
$-$N$-$O$-$V$-----$	not certain
$-$N$-$OV$--$	calm
$-$NO$-$V$----$	not clear

```
− −NOV − − −            to make new
− N − − OV − − −        to turn inside out
− − − − − NOV −         a very bright exploding star
− N − O − V − −         complicated
```

November 2

Present somewhere in this slight confusion,
   Uniquely oblique in its direction,
Zealously look and find the connection,
   Zigzagging unto the ultimate line,
Lingering but briefly on its design.
   Inquisitive minds the truth soon complete.
Nonchalantly you, too, can make ends meet,
   Glimpse opportunely and see the solution.

Explain. Can you find the solution?

November 3

Compose a grammatical and sensible sentence in which all words begin with the same sound and yet none begin with the same letter.

Compose a grammatical and sensible sentence in which all words begin with the same letter and yet none begin with the same sound.

Suggested length for both sentences is around six words.

November 4

Two men at market were selling their apples, one at 30 for $1 and the other at 20 for $1. One day they were both called away when each had 300 apples unsold. These they handed to a friend to sell at 50 for $2. It will be seen that if they had sold their apples

121

separately, they would have fetched $25, but when they were sold together, they fetched only $24. Now, you might ask, what has happened to the missing $1? Surely, 30 for $1 and 20 for $1 is the same as 50 for $2, isn't it?

November 5

Great-uncle George has always enjoyed fireworks, and this year, having just celebrated his birthday, he bought as many rockets as he is years old to mark the occasion. But half of them got damp, the children borrowed a third of the good ones for a private celebration, and the sticks were missing from 21 others. "Never mind," cried the old boy, "it just means that there'll be one for every ten years, instead of one for every year." It was a poor show, though. We'll have a better one when Great-uncle George is 100. When will that be?

November 6

I started two watches at the same time. It turned out that one of them went two mintues per hour too slow, and the other went one minute per hour too fast. When I looked at them again, the faster one was exactly one hour ahead of the other. How long had the watches been running?

November 7

Take the word PRECARIOUSNESS. Delete one letter and re-arrange the remaining letters to make another word. Now delete one letter from this new word and rearrange the remaining letters to make another new word. Keep doing this until there is only one letter left.

November 8

A wooden ruler, 13 inches long, needs only four marks on it so that it can measure any whole number of inches from 1 to 13. The marks are at the 1, 2, 6 and 10 inch positions. From 0 to 1 measures 1 inch, from 0 to 2 measures 2 inches, from 10 to 13 measures 3 inches, from 2 to 6 measures 4 inches, and so on.

On a wooden ruler 36 inches long, what is the smallest number of marks needed so that it can measure any whole number of inches from 1 to 36? And where should the marks be placed?

November 9

On February 18, we saw that the numbers 1 to 9 can be arranged in the form of a square, as shown here, so that each row of numbers has a common total, each column of numbers has the same common total, and the numbers in each of the diagonals have the same total. We called this a "magic square."

$$8\ 1\ 6$$
$$3\ 5\ 7$$
$$4\ 9\ 2$$

The puzzle for February 18 asked you to construct a magic square using the numbers 1 to 16, and the puzzle for July 21 asked for one using the numbers 1 to 25. Now is the time for bigger and better things. Try your hand at creating a magic square using the numbers 1 to 36. All six rows, all six columns, and both diagonals must have the same total.

November 10

Can you recognize words without their E's? Given here are a dozen words from which we have extracted forty-six E's. See if you can work out what the words are by putting back the missing E's. Each word has at least three E's.

a. mr	g. vrgrn
b. rfrnc	h. sntncr
c. rvrnc	i. xcrscnc
d. rsrvdnss	j. lvnss
e. prsss	k. bppprd
f. mrgnc	l. tlmtrd

November 11

The two-digit number 4.5 is equal to the average value of its constituent digits. What other numbers, integral, fractional or decimal, having two or more different digits, display this property?

November 12

A small private zoo contained two freaks of nature, a four-footed bird and a six-legged calf. Altogether in the zoo there were 36 heads and 100 feet. Can you tell us how many birds and how many beasts there were all told in the zoo?

November 13

Here are the names of a dozen countries and regions, all in scrambled form. How many of them can you recognize?

a. rain	g. swan boat
b. pains	h. Englander
c. aspire	i. penalties
d. Maorian	j. resoaping
e. rumbaed	k. Romanians
f. uranism	l. tangerine

November 14

These ten fictitious names are all rearrangements of the names of famous people, past and present. For example, if JESSICA ASANO was in the list, this obscure lady would be translated as one of the most sought-after women of our time, Jackie Onassis. Can you decipher the names of the following ten people?

a. Kevin R. Stroodflane   f. Lory Tanpold
b. Peter Color   g. Gerald Ranoan
c. Dan Fajone   h. Harold Wany
d. Ron Hedfry   i. Bill Canone
e. Eva Stidbet   j. Jill Duchal

November 15

Here are the names of twelve materials and fabrics, but each has been disguised so as to make it look like something else. See what stuff you are made of and find the dozen materials! For example, if UNSLIM was in the list, you should quickly realize that it is really MUSLIN.

a. Alec   g. accoil
b. creep   h. ensate
c. Lenin   i. strowed
d. mined   j. Hellenic
e. olive   k. ungeared
f. saint   l. bargained

November 16

There is a well-known puzzle that runs as follows. An explorer walks one mile south, turns and walks one mile east, turns again and walks one mile due north. He finds himself back where he started. He shoots a bear. What color is the bear? The time-honored answer is 'white', because the explorer must have started at the North Pole. However, someone subsequently made the discovery that the North Pole is not the only starting-point which satisfies the conditions given in the puzzle. Can you think of another spot on the globe from which an explorer could walk one mile south, one mile east, one mile north, and find himself right back where he started from?

November 17

How au fait are you with the titles of old films? If we were to give you this sequence of vowels and dashes: $-O-E-I----E-I--$, would you be able to fill in the missing consonants and arrive at GONE WITH THE WIND? Try your hand at the following ones, all the films coming from the 1930's and 1940's.

a. $-A-A--A--A$
b. $-OO--I----A-A-E$
c. $-O---O---E-E---O---$
d. $--A-E-OA--$
e. $--E--A-E-O---A--$
f. $-E-E-O-E----O--A-$
g. $-EY-A--O$
h. $-I---E-AE-A-$
i. $--I----O-O-E$
j. $--YI---O---O-IO$

November 18

A hiker comes to a fork in the road and doesn't know which way to go to reach his destination. There are two men at the fork, one of whom always tells the truth while the other always lies. The hiker doesn't know which is which, though. He may ask one of the men only one question to find his way. Which man does he ask, and what is the question?

November 19

David Frost, the television interviewer, has a specialty called "crossing jokes." He puts two names together to get a third. If you can solve the crossing jokes below, you may be lucky enough to get invited to appear on one of his programs . . . . On the other hand, you may not. Anyway, try these three jokes.

a. Cross a cowboy with a gourmet and you get a . . . . .

b. Cross Jimmy Durante with an employment agency and you get a . . . . .

c. Cross a zebra with a jungle dweller and you get . . . . .

November 20

Below are the names of a dozen rivers, but the letters in each have meandered about until the rivers are not instantly recognizable. Can you put the letters back into their correct orders, and so come up with the twelve rivers?

a. rode   g. line

b. nova   h. namer

c. froth   i. oiler

d. heron   j. shirty

e. unshod   k. sintered

f. relined   l. Havanans

November 21

On several occasions, we have seen that the letters CCCCCCC can be interpreted as The Seven Seas. Now see if you can make sense of the seven clues given here.

a. $\dfrac{1}{8}$

b. $\dfrac{C}{\text{exams}}$

c. sand-p-Needles

d. $\dfrac{\text{head}}{D}$

e. $\dfrac{M}{7}$

f. $\dfrac{\text{Francis}}{\text{ehenge}}$

g. $\dfrac{M}{\text{aco}}$

November 22

A recent newspaper item ran as follows:

> The higher court today vacated the injunction restraining the police from interfering with the pickets opposing the distribution of pamphlets attacking the Anti-Tobacco League.

You needn't be a lawyer to answer these questions:

a. Were the police pleased?
b. Were the distributors pleased?
d. Were the cigarette companies pleased?
e. Was the Anti-Tobacco League pleased?

November 23

What, if anything, can you deduce from these five statements?

a. Promise-breakers are untrustworthy
b. Wine-drinkers are very communicative
c. A man who keeps his promises is honest
d. No teetotallers are pawnbrokers
e. One can always trust a very communicative person

November 24

Using the figure 4 four times, and simple mathematical symbols, the number 12 can be represented as follows:

$$\frac{44 + 4}{4}$$

And 15, 16 and 17 can be represented by the following expressions:

$$\frac{44}{4} + 4 \qquad 4 + 4 + 4 + 4 \qquad 4 \times 4 + \frac{4}{4}$$

Using the same approach, can you devise representations for the numbers from 0 to 10? You ought to be able to stick with addition signs, subtraction signs, multiplication signs, and division signs.

November 25

A commonly heard story is the one about the small sick boy in an upstairs bedroom, who hears his mother coming up the stairs with some reading material for him. He calls out to her, "Why are you bringing the book that I do not want to be read to out of up for?" This simple little question just happens to end with five consecutive prepositions! And didn't our teachers drum into us that sentences shouldn't end in prepositions? Goodness knows what a teacher's reaction to *five* prepositions at the end of a sentence would be! However, we wonder if you can do better than the sick boy. Can you dream up a reasonable sentence that ends with more than five prepositions?

November 26

Which is longer: 666 yards or 3 furlongs plus 200 inches?
Which is longer: 666 minutes or one-fourteenth of a week?

Which is longer: 666 millimeters or 2 feet?
Which is longer: 666 days or 95 weeks?
Which is longer: 666 inches or 55 feet?
Which is longer: 666 hours or 28 days?

November 27

Here is a rather simple question with a "yes" or "no" answer. It just happens to be phrased in a roundabout way, but that shouldn't disturb you if you can find a way to reduce it to its fundamentals. This can be done in three steps, leading to your rephrasing the question in such simple terms that the answer is immediately apparent. Now go ahead.

"If the puzzle you solved before you solved the puzzle you solved after you solved the puzzle you solved before you solved this one, was harder than the puzzle you solved after you solved the puzzle you solved before you solved this one, was the puzzle you solved before you solved this one harder than this one?"

Yes or no?

November 28

Not so long ago, I was stuck in a very slow-moving traffic jam. To relieve the boredom, I started playing a game with car license plates. Using just the letters on car license plates, I tried to find a word using the letters, in order, from each plate I saw. For example, NWB 347L made me think of SNOWBALL. The digits on the license plate are to be ignored, you see. Here are ten plates I spotted. What words can you make from their letters?

NKP 234T   HPN 794D
LKM 368H   HLG 842T

```
PFD 473R    LYH 974G
RMD 557B    TLD 247H
SCG 694E    PCC 368L
```

November 29

A printer had an order for 10,000 bill forms per month, but each month the name of the particular month had to be altered. That is, he printed 10,000 with JANUARY on, 10,000 with FEBRUARY on, 10,000 with MARCH on, and so on. As the particular types with which these words were to be printed had to be specially obtained and were expensive, he only purchased just enough movable types to enable him, by interchanging them, to print in turn the whole of the months of the year. How many separate types did he purchase? Of course, the words were printed throughout in capital letters, as shown.

November 30

Using the letters of ANDREW, make three six-letter words. Using five of the six letters of ANDREW, make three five-letter words. Using four of the six letters of ANDREW, make ten four-letter words. Using three of the six letters of ANDREW, make ten three-letter words. Oh yes, just one other thing. In all the words you make, you must ensure that there is a W.

December 1

Following are clues for ten words. Against each clue is an indication of the word's length, and also where the letters DEC occur in the word. See if you can sort out what the complete words are. As an example, if the clue was "hesitant" and the letter pattern was ——DEC————, you should be able to work out that the answer is INDECISIVE.

DEC − − −   ten years
DEC − − − − −   to beautify
D − E − C −   to soak
− − DEC − −   a part of some motorcycles
− − DEC − − −   ornamented
− − − DE − C − − −   to deign
− − − D − − EC − − − −   preference
DE − − − − − C   tyrannical
DE − − C −   infer
− − − DE − − − − − C −   a monster invented by
                              Lewis Carroll

December 2

Examine each of the five sentences below. What is unusual about
them? They all display a special property that shouldn't be too
difficult to spot.

a. Sums are not set as a test on Erasmus
b. Stella won no wallets
c. Eva, can I stab live, evil bats in a cave?
d. I maim nine men in Miami
e. Marge lets Norah see Sharon's telegram

December 3

See if you can complete words by putting three letters on each
side of the following twelve combinations.

a. ural   e. caut
b. ocia   f. hest
c. upul   g. ment
d. cina   h. idel

132

i. redi   k. olut
j. dpec   l. epho

December 4

Disguised below are a dozen famous entertainers. Their twelve first names have been jumbled up to form other words; these are in the two columns on the left. Their twelve last names have also been jumbled up to form other words; these are in the two columns on the right. Can you pair off the words to find the twelve well-known names from the world of showbiz, past and present? For example, if LACE was in the left columns and ENSUINGS was in the right columns, you would pair them off to find ALEC GUINNESS.

and	lane	genre	roomer
Ayr	Elmer	heron	unshod
elm	loner	Metro	larches
brut	scare	Antrim	enrobing
cork	barbar	Audrey	ancestral
Dane	resent	Borneo	tardiness

December 5

Playing with his new electronic calculator, which, among other features, has an exceptionally long display, the absent-minded professor discovered by chance a number that, when he transferred the unit digit from the right-hand end to the left-hand end, became the original number multiplied by that digit. Unfortunately, just as he was about to jot down this remarkable discovery, the calculator's batteries failed. All that the professor could remember was that the original number began 10112 . . . . . Can you reconstruct the original number for the professor?

December 6

Find words which contain the following letter sequences.

a. diffid g. rammar
b. dissid h. reller
c. millim i. selles
d. narran j. sesses
e. nessen k. sottos
f. niffin l. taccat

Notice that all of these six-letter sequences read the same backwards as forwards.

December 7

When three quite ordinary words are "telescoped" together, like those given here, it is not always easy to recognize them, even though their letters are in the correct order. For example, given NONCABLEROPE, would you be able to spot that it was made up from ABLE, CROP and NONE? Now try those given here, bearing in mind that each is made up from three four-letter words.

a. GROVEMENSHIP f. SUNTEARINGLY
b. COUNTERHAILS g. MINISTETSONS
c. MEDICOHEMALS h. COHAMPTONESE
d. COMPUTERITES i. WEATHERSTARS
e. SUPERBOARDED j. REAUTOMERGED

December 8

Mary had a tiny lamb,
 Its wool was pallid as snow,

And any spot that Mary did walk
   This lamb would always go;
This lamb did follow Mary to school,
   Although against a law;
How girls and boys did laugh and play,
   That lamb in class all saw.

What zany charm can you find in this? Think!

December 9

The word CHEWED contains within itself two pronouns, HE and WE. What common six-letter word, a noun, contains five different pronouns, each showing up as a solid word in its spelling? There is another common noun, one of eight letters, from the letters of which at least 17 different pronouns can be formed by proper letter selection and shuffling. Name the word.

December 10

Can you give the sum of all the whole numbers that can be formed with the four digits 1, 2, 3 and 4? That is, the addition of all such numbers as 1,234, 1,324, 4,321, 3,421, etc. You can, of course, write them all out and make the addition, but the interest lies in finding a very simple rule for the sum of all the numbers that can be made with four different digits selected in every possible way, but with zero included.

December 11

Two six-sided dice are marked with 12 different whole numbers in such a way that any number from 1 to 36 inclusive can be given when both are thrown and the values of the two face-up sides added. What is the lowest possible value that the highest single face can show in order to produce this effect?

December 12

Which is heavier: 1000 kilograms or 1 ton?

Which is longer: 250 centimeters or 8 feet?

Which is larger: 3 raised to the 5th power or 5 raised to the 3rd power?

Which is hotter: zero degrees Centigrade or zero degrees Fahrenheit?

Which are there more of: ounces in a ton or inches in a kilometer?

Which is colder: -40 degrees Centigrade or -40 degrees Fahrenheit?

December 13

In this puzzle, the answer to each of the first parts is reversed to give the answer to each of the second parts.

a. reverse a card game to cloth
b. reverse a feast to prize
c. invert feet to exchange
d. invert praise and get twofold
e. invert disposition for judgment
f. invert growths and get fodder
g. reverse a pace and get the favorites
h. invert a first appearance and get piped
i. reverse a certainty for fasteners
j. invert malice to exist

December 14

Five friends sat around a table sharing a quick snack. Each had a drink, a sandwich, and dessert. Abner and Mr. Clapton drank tea. Billy and Mr. Boone drank coffee. Mr. Arkwright drank milk.

Abner and Mr. Drayton had bologna sandwiches, while Chuck and Mr. Arkwright had a ham sandwich each. Chuck and Mr. Entwistle ate eclairs, while Dwight and Mr. Arkwright ate pie. One man had a sherbet. The waiter noticed that he never served two of anything to men who were seated next to one another. Who had the cheese sandwich and what did Ed have?

December 15

The patterns for eight words have the same letters at the front and back, and are presented below. You are to supply a word that forms a larger word when inserted into the central position. The number of dashes indicates the number of letters in the core word. For example, given the pattern ma———ma, you would supply the word HAT, making MAHATMA.

a. en———en   e. re————er
b. es————es   f. st———st
c. Ic—————ic   g. st————st
d. ing———ing   h. tor———tor

December 16

Shackleton, Campbell, Garfield, and Colson make up a flight crew—pilot, copilot, navigator and engineer—but not necessarily in that order. Assign the right man to the right job on the basis of the following information, some of which may not be of any use to you.

a. The pilot and copilot are good friends
b. Shackleton and Colson are not good friends
c. The engineer's wife is a passenger
d. Shackleton and Colson do not wear glasses . . .
e. . . . but I'm not sure about the other two
f. Only Garfield and Colson are married

g. Garfield had lunch with the copilot
h. The pilot doesn't wear glasses . . .
i. . . . but the navigator does
j. The navigator is engaged to the stewardess
k. The stewardess is good-looking

December 17

In the following 26-word sentence, the initial letters of successive words constitute the entire alphabet in correct order. To write such a sentence, maintaining a reasonable continuity of thought, requires skill. See if you can match the sentence here.

"At Bombay, ceremonial demonstrations, Eastern fakirs (godless heathen Indians) juggle knives, leaving me nervously obedient, praying quietly religion shall temper un-Christian villainy, winning xenophobic yogi zealots."

December 18

How familiar are you with the names of film and television cowboys? If we were to give you this sequence of vowels and dashes: —A———I——O—, would you be able to fill in the missing consonants and arrive at MATT DILLON? Try your hand at the following ones.

a. —A—E—I——
b. ——EYE——E
c. —U————A——I—Y
d. —O—A—O———A——I—Y
e. ——O——O
f. ——E—O—E—A——E—
g. —O——YYA—E—
h. —E——A————I———

i. — O — — UA — — I — —

j. — YA — — EA — —

December 19

In the English and Russian alphabets, the capital letters A, E, K, M, O and T are equivalent, while the English letters N, R, S, U and Y are represented by the Cyrillic symbols H, P, C, Y and B. The Russian equivalents of the remaining 15 English letters are not Roman characters. Using the 11 letters above, what is the longest English word whose Russian cipher equivalent is also an English word?

December 20

Find the missing letter in this array:

G O R P

A L I H

M A ? A

S A T N

December 21

If Uganda is represented by UGA (UG and A), what placenames are indicated by the following?

a. &/or RA   d. LI a

b. LAFND   e. IO5P

c. $\overset{C}{GO}$ f. $\overset{L}{\underset{G}{}}$ Capri

December 22

HELL is a peculiar word. Change the first letter to B, and you get BELL. Change the second letter to A, and you get HALL. Change the third letter to A, and you get HEAL. Change the fourth letter to M, and you get HELM. There are very few words where each letter in turn can be changed so as to make another word. And it becomes more difficult as you try and effect the same process with longer words. However, five and six-letter examples do exist. See if you can find them.

December 23

Only one 5-letter word is found in verse————————, Chapter —————, Book of——————————, in the Bible. What is it?

The numbers of dashes equal the number of letters in the words concerned.

December 24

Christmas Eve

Each of the items displayed here represents a familiar word, name or phrase connected in some way with Christmas. For example, INWG & INDG can be recognized as "wining and dining." Now have fun with the others.

a. stel	f. twer
b. dereer	g. CME pi pi pi
c. br Y	pi pi pi
d. gstocks	h. cLes
e. $\dfrac{\text{Red Black}}{\text{S}}$	i. $\dfrac{\text{Red Yellow}}{\text{AL}}$ hi hi hi hi hi hi hi hi hi

December 25

Christmas Day; Noel; Xmas; Yule

1. Delete one letter from the word CHRISTMAS and rearrange the remaining letters to make a new word. Delete one letter from the new word and rearrange the remaining letters to make another new word. Keep doing this until there is just one letter left.
2. Rearrange the letters in the following phrase: AN OLDTIME CHRISTMAS and come up with a particularly apt seasonal comment.
3. Rearrange the letters in the phrase CHRISTMAS TIME to make a phrase which describes what CHRISTMAS does to children.
4. Take the three words NOEL, XMAS and YULE. Rearrange the 12 letters to make a group of three four-letter words. Repeat this twice, ensuring that none of the words is used more than once.

December 26

When three quite ordinary words are "telescoped" together, like those given here, it is not always easy to recognize them, even though their letters are in the correct order. For example, given NONCABLEROPE, would you be able to spot that it was made up from NONE, ABLE and CROP? Now try the ten given here, bearing in mind that each is made up from three four-letter words.

a. CHRISTMASITH   f. REINDEERISED
b. SEASONALREST   g. THELASTMONTH
c. WINTERTOASTS   h. WIBWESTTEEKS
d. COSYDECEMBER   i. SUPERTINKERS
e. THISYEARSEND   j. OVERRENTALLY

December 27

Insert in the blank space between each of the two matched syllables below a syllable (of any length) that will make one word out of the first syllable, and another out of the second.

a. ham — — — — — tuce
b. hand — — — — — body
c. house — — — — — man
d. mis — — — — — tain
e. pre — — — — — ence
f. prow — — — — — ence
g. pur — — — — — able
h. sun — — — — — tee
i. tas — — — — — rant
j. war — — — — — well

December 28

On November 17, we quizzed you on the titles of some films from the 1930's and 1940's. Well, here are some more. As an example, given this sequence of vowels and dashes: — O — E — I — — — — E — I — —, would you be able to spot that it was GONE WITH THE WIND?

a. — — E — A — — E — E — A — — O —

b. $-A-IO-A--E--E-$

c. $--E-A--O--U-A---U$

d. $-O---I--E--O-----$

e. $--E-OA-I----E--IE-$

f. $-I-I-E--A-E$

g. $-U-I-YO---E-OU--Y$

h. $-O--A-$

i. $-OO--I----A-A-E$

j. $--E-I---EE-$

k. $A-I---A---EO-E-A$

December 29

Using the letters of WILLIAM EWART GLADSTONE, we see that it can be anagrammed into the following relevant phrases:

a. Wilt tear down all images
b. Wild agitator means well
c. Will mislead a great town
d. We want a mild legislator

But we're sure you can do just as well. Try your hand and see if you can devise four more anagrams on this politician's name.

December 30

What a swindle this book is! I thought it was a puzzle book, but there are more jokes in it than any other kind of thing. So thought George. He was unhappy. He continued complaining, "It has as many magic tricks as it has logic puzzles and algebra problems put together."

Said his father, "But, son, there are twice as many algebra problems, which you like, as there are mazes."

"That's true," acknowledged the critical George, "but you know that I don't care much for either mazes or riddles, so you'll see why I'm grumbling when I say there are more of these two types combined than there are magic tricks, and that is saying a lot—more than 20 percent of the items in the book are magic tricks. And another point, you know that I like logic puzzles, but here there are twice as many riddles as logic puzzles. And don't forget that there are six stories; that doesn't leave room for many of the kinds that I like. I say it is a swindle!"

How bad was it? What are the minimum numbers of algebra problems and logic puzzles in the collection?

December 31

And just to finish off the year, rearrange the letters of HOG-MANAY to make another English word.

Solutions

JANUARY 1
janitor, jasmine, jargon, jubilant, Trojan, jacinth, Jacobean, panjandrum, adjutant, conjugation

JANUARY 2
(a) $5 + 5 + 5 = 15$ (b) $89 + 9 = 98$
(c) $23 + 23 + 23 + 23 = 92$ (d) $999 + 1 = 1000$

JANUARY 3
John Wayne, Warren Beatty, Peter Fonda, Ginger Rogers, Paul Newman, Clark Gable, Warren Oates, Clint Eastwood, Charlton Heston, Yul Brynner

JANUARY 4
(a) Much Ado about Nothing (b) World without end, amen
(c) A frame-up (d) All in one (e) Six of one, half a dozen of another (f) Square meal

JANUARY 5
If I walk 26 steps, I need 30 seconds; and if I walk 34 steps, I need only 18 seconds. Multiply 30 by 34 and 26 by 18, and we get 1020 and 468. Divide the difference (552) by the difference between 30 seconds and 18 seconds (that is, 12 seconds). The answer is 46, the number of steps in the stairway, which descends at the rate of 1 step in $1\frac{1}{2}$ seconds. The speed at which I walk on the stairs doesn't affect the question, as the step from which I alight will reach the bottom at a given moment, whatever I do in the meantime.

JANUARY 6
Get lost! A-OK! Groovy! Outasight!

JANUARY 7
12344—glass; 11232—llama; 12123—cocoa; 12132—mamba; 12133—amass; 12213—allay; 12231—seeds; 12233—cooee; 12312—verve; 12313—ended; 12323—ceded; 12331—tweet; 12332—manna; 11231—eerie; 12113—lulls; 12131—rarer; 12311—fluff; 12232—error; 12322—levee; 12112—mamma

JANUARY 8

The taxi driver's number was 121.

JANUARY 9

Fox-ox, flute-lute, brim-rim, bark-ark, smelt-melt, arise-rise, flag-lag, Amabell-Mabel-Abel, complaint-complain, covert-cover, mark-mar, hide-hid, open-ope

JANUARY 10

To begin with, there were 20 people, and each received $6. 15 people (that is, 5 fewer) would have received $8 each. But 24 (4 more) appeared and only received $5 each. The amount distributed each week was $120.

JANUARY 11

The Jacksons sold 220 more papers than the Saunderses. The original number of papers was 1020.

JANUARY 12

$9725 + 4925 + 21350 + 61850 = 97850$, and 4096 is 4 raised to the 6th power.

JANUARY 13

Scar-trig-lens, moon-arms-trap, ryes-folk-tsar, gnat-reel-pies, only-swig-parr, fort-yams-beer, sale-that-beer, only-xyst-gone, fore-type-lass

JANUARY 14

a. deed   b. level   c. redder   d. noon   e. sexes   f. reviver
g. sagas   h. civic   i. dewed   j. rotator

JANUARY 15

Vile, evil, veil, Levi, live, Ivel

JANUARY 16

Common sense tells you that if each missile has a chance of missing the target, then there is a chance that all four missiles will miss. Also, that the target may be hit by one, two, three or all four missiles. Since each missile has 3 chances in 4 of missing the target, the probability that all four will miss is:

$$\tfrac{3}{4} \times \tfrac{3}{4} \times \tfrac{3}{4} \times \tfrac{3}{4} = \tfrac{81}{256}.$$

The probability that the target will not be missed is:
$$1 - \tfrac{81}{256},$$
or

$$\tfrac{175}{256}.$$

So, Johnny was wrong.

JANUARY 17

$$13 \times 62 = 31 \times 26 \qquad 23 \times 64 = 32 \times 46$$
$$13 \times 93 = 31 \times 39 \qquad 34 \times 86 = 43 \times 68$$
$$14 \times 82 = 41 \times 28 \qquad 36 \times 84 = 63 \times 48$$

JANUARY 18
Wellington

JANUARY 19
Fox, never, stung, whiz; Unfrozen, vex, wights

JANUARY 20
Bag, chid, chide, chin, chintz, die, dim, din, dint, fag, gab, hid, hide, hie, him, hint, ion, jot, join, joint, mid, mint, not, nut, out, snide, stoic, stun, sty, ton, tun, tunic

JANUARY 21
a. peep b. toot c. solos d. tenet e. kook f. Shahs g. defied h. refer i. booby j. radar

JANUARY 22
8.000000

JANUARY 23
The past tenses of the eight verbs all rhyme with TAUT.

JANUARY 24
Answer number 1: None, if the dead blackbird falls off and the rest fly away, scared by the shot. Answer number 2: 24, if the roof is so flat that the dead blackbird doesn't fall off and the shot is fired from so far away that the rest of the blackbirds aren't scared away by the shot. Answer number 3: One,

if the roof is so flat that the dead blackbird doesn't fall off and the shot is loud enough to scare the live blackbirds. Answer number 4: 23, if the roof is so steep that the dead one falls off and the shot is so quiet that the live ones don't fly away. Things are seldom simple, are they?

JANUARY 25

Dane, dene, dine, done, dune, dyne. There are probably other equally valid solutions.

JANUARY 26

If he can cycle a mile in three minutes with the wind, he could go $1\frac{1}{3}$ miles in four minutes. He returns against the wind in the same four minutes, so he could go $2\frac{1}{3}$ miles in eight minutes, with the wind helping exactly half the time and hindering him for the other half. So, the wind can be ignored, and we conclude that on a windless day he could go $2\frac{1}{3}$ miles in eight minutes, or one mile in 3 and $\frac{3}{7}$ minutes. It is incorrect to halve the total time to obtain an average speed, because one way the wind helps the cyclist for three minutes, and the other way it hinders him for four minutes. So, if you said $3\frac{1}{2}$ minutes, you were wrong.

JANUARY 27

a. You are not a doctor b. Dictionaries are valuable c. No unselfish people save bottle tops

JANUARY 28

Cold, cord, word, ward, warm. Evil, Emil, emit, smit, suit, suet, sues, dues, does, doer, door, moor, mood, good

JANUARY 29

17531908 + 7088062 = 24619970

JANUARY 30

900 picnickers started out with 100 wagons, 9 picnickers to each wagon

JANUARY 31

Burma, Chile, Western Samoa, Senegal, Costa Rica. Philippines is not a valid answer for the fourth one!

FEBRUARY 1
Febrile, freebooter, inferable, defendable or defensible, unfeasible, fieldboots, fingerboard, firebrand, forebode, forecabin

FEBRUARY 2
If you pronounce GH as in TOUGH, O as in WOMEN, and TI as in EMOTION, it follows that GHOTI must be pronounced FISH!

FEBRUARY 3
a. Once upon a time b. Not before time c. Two peas in a pod d. Just between friends e. Rin Tin Tin f. Thunder and lightning g. Sovereign h. Bingo i. The third of February j. Cover story

FEBRUARY 4
The numbers from ONE to TEN can all be spelled out in order by groups of adjacent letters.

FEBRUARY 5
Chloe lives two miles from Bertha, and Hattie Benn is the oldest of the girls.

FEBRUARY 6
If you turn the list upside down and read it in a mirror, the words will stay the same. Or, put another way, each of the words is made up from letters which are symmetrical with respect to a horizontal line passing through their centers.

FEBRUARY 7
a. Ratio b. ochre c. elegy d. yearn e. nerve f. extra g. awful h. laugh i. Halma j. addle k. epoch l. Hades m. sigma n. adept o. tired. The middle letters spell THE ARTFUL DODGER.

FEBRUARY 8
Call the children A, B, C, D and E in order of their weights, A being the lightest and E the heaviest. A and B (the two lightest) together weigh 114 pounds. D and E (the two heaviest) together weigh 129 pounds. These four together weigh 243 pounds, which, deducted from the weight of all five,

303 pounds, gives us the weight of C, 60 pounds. (To obtain the total weight of 303 pounds, add all the pairs together and divide by 4, since each child was weighed four times.) The lightest and next lightest but one weighed 115 pounds — that is, A and C. Since C is 60 pounds, A must be 55 pounds. The rest is now quite simple. The children's individual weights turn out to be 55, 59, 60, 63 and 66 pounds.

FEBRUARY 9
Bikini, dividing, illicit, inclining, libidinist, limiting, minikin, minimising, Mississippi, Philippic, timidity, visibility

FEBRUARY 10
There are 212 different dates in this century complying with the conditions, excluding such cases as 25.4.00, 20.5.00 and 10.10.00. The most fruitful year was 1924, when there were seven cases: 24.1.24, 12.2.24, 8.3.24, 6.4.24, 4.6.24, 3.8.24, and 2.12.24.

FEBRUARY 11
Excommunication. Thus:

E	10	100	0	1000	1000	UNI	100	AT	X	N
E	X	C	0	M	M	UNI	C	AT	10	N

FEBRUARY 12
Abstemiously

FEBRUARY 13
$5\frac{1}{2}$ minutes past two o'clock. Even more accurately, it was five and five-elevenths minutes past two o'clock.

FEBRUARY 14
Agreeable, bountiful, constant, dutiful, easy, faithful, gallant, honorable, ingenious, just, kind, loyal, mild, noble, obliging, prudent, quiet, rich, secret, true, valiant, wise, young, zealous

FEBRUARY 15
The first sequence of numbers is in reverse alphabetical order. The second sequence of numbers represents the chimes of a clock that strikes once on the half-hours, so the next four

numbers are 1, 4, 1 and 5. Eight 8's can be arranged so to add up to 1000: 888 + 88 + 8 + 8 + 8.

FEBRUARY 16
Spoons, snoops; sinned, Dennis; sloops, spools; denier, reined; steels, sleets; sports, strops

FEBRUARY 17
Here is one magic square using the numbers 1 to 16.

```
 1 15 14  4
12  6  7  9
 8 10 11  5
13  3  2 16
```

FEBRUARY 18
The initial letters of the four lines quoted spell out the word WHAT. So, the question is also the answer. WHAT is the essence, substance, or distinctive quality of this passage. WHAT must strike every reader of these lines.

FEBRUARY 19

```
V O T E R
O C H R E
T H E R E
E R R E D
R E E D Y
```

FEBRUARY 20
a. Conversation b. desperation c. softheartedness d. therapeutics e. punishment f. disconsolate

FEBRUARY 21
Spark, park, ark

FEBRUARY 22
a. Sanatorium, sanitarium b. descry, decry c. mendicity, mendacity d. adjure, abjure e. abrade, upbraid f. discomfit,

discomfort g. venal, venial h. indite, indict i. complacent, complaisant j. biennial, biannual

FEBRUARY 23

546250 + 546250 + 593750 = 1686250. This isn't quite perfect as N and R (7 and 2) are interchangeable.

FEBRUARY 24

Black, block, clock, chock, chick, chink, chine, whine, white. Chine is an old word for a backbone.

FEBRUARY 25

The potato weighed 11 ounces, the orange 7 ounces, the apple 5 ounces, the tomato 3 ounces, and the banana 2 ounces.

FEBRUARY 26

The numbers of votes polled for each of the candidates was as follows: Democrat 15,530; Republican 15,350; Independent 14,070; and Socialist 9780. All that is necessary is to add the sum of the three majorities (7390) to the total poll (54,730), giving 62,120, and then to divide by 4, which gives 15,530 as the number of Democrat votes polled. The votes for the other candidates can be found by deducting the successive majorities from 15,530.

FEBRUARY 27

All twelve months have twenty-eight days. Some have a few more as well!

FEBRUARY 28

TWENTYNINE is the only number composed entirely of as many straight lines as the number itself indicates; that is, 29. If the number is spelled with a hyphen, TWENTY-NINE, the modification necessary is to use a Y with two strokes rather than the three-stroke Y used here.

MARCH 1

Margin, marten, fulmar, amateur, Martinmas, summary, miniature, impartial, nightmare, commander

MARCH 2

The man was given five 2¢ stamps, fifty 1¢ stamps, and eight 5¢ stamps.

MARCH 3

a. Bass b. chub c. dab d. hake e. ray f. cod g. eel h. ling i. pike j. roach

MARCH 4

The missing words are ENTRANT, STRANGE, LANTERN and ENGORGE.

MARCH 5

A nod is as good as a wink to a blind horse.

MARCH 6

If the same 20 questions are put to both spectators, the chances are that they will give truthful answers to 12 of them, contradictory answers to 7 (3 plus 4), and untruthful answers to one. So, for every 13 times they agree on an answer, it is likely to be incorrect on one occasion. So, the odds are 12 to 1 on that it was actually the Senate Majority Leader.

MARCH 7

a. King Kong b. hovercraft c. head over heels in love d. Stranger in Paradise e. Home on the Range f. Island in the Sun g. The Pied Piper h. wined and dined i. Far from the Madding Crowd j. Dover sole

MARCH 8

Charm and height. April can be rearranged to give prial; and May gives both Amy and yam.

MARCH 9

9 links and 15 links

MARCH 10

Animal, lamina; drawer, reward; spacer, recaps; tenner, rennet; deliver, reviled; desserts, stressed

Black Horse, White Horse, Green Dragon, Black Swan, Coach and Horses, White Swan

MARCH 12
The messenger is a truth-teller. If the native in the distance lived on the western side of the island, and was a truthteller, he would say so. If, on the other hand, he lived on the eastern side of the island, and was therefore a liar, he would say the same thing.

MARCH 13
a. The fiendish spectre haunts the manor each night b. Never trifle with strange beasts c. Genuine antique dealers seldom deal in replicas d. A recipe if perfect lists all the ingredients e. A tornado can cause alarming results when it hits a town f. In general, granite rocks are the hardest ones

MARCH 14
Fig, date, apple, peach, nectarine, melon, pear, orange, olive, gourd, lemon, raisin

MARCH 15
Probably the 16 commonest names are these: Amos, Chris, Dora, Ed, Eric, Erica, Freda, Homer, Horace, Ida, Marie, Oscar, Rhoda, Rosa, Rose, and Sadie

MARCH 16
$1011^2 = 1022121$. If the calculator display was viewed upside down throughout the operation, the viewer would see 1101 being squared to produce, correctly, 1212201.

MARCH 17
It is clear that O'Malley wanted to give the mother twice as much as the daughter, and the son twice as much as the mother. It is a simple matter then to give the daughter one-seventh, the mother two-sevenths, and the son four-sevenths.

MARCH 18
On the Saturday morning, £1 was worth 8 francs, or 4 marks, or 96 pesetas.

154

MARCH 19

ARMY—MYNA—NAVY is the shortest such chain. A myna is a talking bird.

MARCH 20

The prices quoted were for house-numbers at 12 cents per digit. A number 6 digit cost me 12 cents.

MARCH 21

$$\frac{5832}{17496}=\frac{1}{3} \qquad \frac{4392}{17568}=\frac{1}{4}$$

$$\frac{2769}{13843}=\frac{1}{5} \qquad \frac{2943}{17658}=\frac{1}{6}$$

$$\frac{2394}{16758}=\frac{1}{7} \qquad \frac{3187}{25496}=\frac{1}{8}$$

$$\frac{6381}{57429}=\frac{1}{9}$$

MARCH 22

Call the three men A, B and C. A and his wife cross the river. A returns. B's wife and C's wife cross the river. A's wife returns. B and C cross the river. B and his wife return. A and B cross the river. C's wife returns. A's wife and B's wife cross the river. C returns. C and his wife cross the river.

MARCH 23

The only other four-digit number complying with the conditions is 9801. 98 plus 01 is 99, and 99 squared is 9801.

MARCH 24

a. Nevada b. Maine c. Maryland d. Washington e. Minnesota f. Rhode Island g. Indiana h. Pennsylvania i. Rhode Island j. South Carolina

MARCH 25

a. Glenda b. Marian and Marina c. Brenda d. Ingrid e. Bertha f. Esther and Hester g. Melissa h. Loretta i. Deirdre j. Mildred k. Tabitha l. Rosetta m. Rosaline n. Rosalind o. Hortensia p. Geraldine

MARCH 26

840 is more remarkable. It can be divided by 1, 2, 3, 4, 5, 6, 7, 8, 10, 12, 14, 15, 20, 21, 24, 28, 30, 35, 40, 42, 56, 60, 70, 84, 105, 120, 140, 168, 210, 280, 420 and 840. Phew!

MARCH 27
The widow received $205.13.

MARCH 28
a. Leonardo (artist and scientist) b. Newton (scientist and mathematician) c. Aristotle (philosopher and scientist) d. Keaton (Buster Keaton was a silent film star, and Diane Keaton is the 1970's film star).

MARCH 29
Four customers will be satisfied, if there were 80 (or 140, or 200 . . .) rabbits originally. There is no way that a fifth customer can receive six rabbits plus one-sixth of the remainder.

MARCH 30
Nowhere — now here. The two rearrangements are WHEREON and EREWHON, the latter being the title of a utopian novel by Samuel Butler.

MARCH 31
a. Metaphysicians b. remuneration c. families d. earnestness e. steaminess

APRIL 1
The radius is t, so the circumference is 2.pi.t. The runner runs around n times, for a total distance of 2.pi.t.n miles. Since he drinks s quarts per mile, the total number of quarts drunk is 2.pi.t.n.s. These factors can be put in any order, so they can be made to read 2.pi.n.t.s. And everyone knows that 2 pints is just one quart!

APRIL 2
A private, late on parade,
Carelessly shouldered a spade.
Cried sarge: "Stand at ease,
Present arms, if you please.
Private Glass has a new kind of blade!"

APRIL 3
a. Athens b. Naples c. Manila d. Regina e. Tangier f. Tangiers g. Trieste h. Tijuana i. Dresden j. Cremona k.

Denver l. Detroit m. Reading n. San Diego o. Greenwich
p. Leningrad

APRIL 4

a. I'm ready come hell or high water b. He's filthy rich c.
He's dressed to kill and generous to a fault d. She was left
high and dry e. Faint heart ne'er won fair lady

APRIL 5

The unique answer is $570140 \times 6 = 3420840$.

APRIL 6

The musician is Bertram Fuller. Here is an outline of the solution, giving only the successive conclusions: Dwight is Mr.
Hooper, Clint is the accountant, Bertram is the musician, Ambrose is the priest, Dwight Hooper is the doctor, Ambrose is
not Mr. Grimm, Mr. Eastwood is Ambrose, Clint is not Mr.
Fuller, Clint is Mr. Grimm (the accountant), and Bertram
Fuller is the musician.

APRIL 7

The two halves of the name WORDSWORTH occur in the last
line: . . . words of worth . . . The first letter of each of the ten
lines spells out the name WORDSWORTH. The content of the
lines themselves comprises a thumbnail sketch of Wordsworth.
The use of the word "excurison" in the penultimate line is a
reference to Wordsworth's work "The Excursion" (1814).

APRIL 8

There are 1296 different rectangles in all, 204 of which are
squares, counting the square board itself as one, and 1092
rectangles which are not squares.

APRIL 9

Only five other fractions of three digits over three digits produce the same quantity when an improper cancellation is made
between the "units" digit of the numerator and the "tens" digit
of the denominator. These are: $\frac{133}{931}$, $\frac{149}{894}$, $\frac{159}{795}$, $\frac{233}{932}$ and $\frac{249}{498}$. Of
these, only one results in a fraction of the same form which
can be improperly cancelled again to produce the correct result. The student's second fraction was $\frac{249}{498}$, which he reduced

157

to $\frac{24}{48}$. So far, so good. But further cancellation, to $\frac{2}{8}$, proved his method wrong and his teacher right.

APRIL 10

The check was $31.63. He received $63.31. After he spent 5¢, he had $63.26, twice the amount of his check.

APRIL 11

a. Austin   b. Wolseley   c. Maserati   d. Bristol   e. Rolls Royce f. Jowett   g. Triumph Spitfire   h. Datsun   i. Escort   J. Cortina   k. Citroen   l. Renault   m. Chevrolet   n. Sunbeam   o. Oldsmobile   p. Aston Martin   q. Van Den Plas   r. Mini   s. Reliant   t. Daimler

APRIL 12

She started off with $99.98. She spent $49.99.

APRIL 13

Bleed, Larne, erode, ended, deeds

APRIL 14

a. Guyana   b. America   c. Afghanistan   (or any of the others with the same ending)   d. Jordan   e. Indonesia   f. New Zealand   g. Hungary   h. Great Britain or Mauritania   i. Philippines

APRIL 15

a. adder   b. chain   c. fills   d. mills   e. cobra   f. banjo   g. cheer h. sneer   i. sheer   j. pecan

APRIL 16

yea, à pied, sundae, weigh, quai, ok, soleil, dossier, Beaujolais, sobriquet, bay, chez

APRIL 17

The fewest plus and minus signs is 3. This is the solution:
$$123 - 45 - 67 + 89 = 100$$

APRIL 18

a. American Graffiti   b. Chinatown   c. Bonnie and Clyde   d. Rollerball   e. Star Wars   f. The Exorcist   g. The Way We Were h. Saturday Night Fever   i. Shampoo   j. The Great Gatsby

158

APRIL 19

The words are the shortest ones from which the names of the numbers, from ONE to TWENTY, can be spelled out. Numbers above TWENTY may be added to the list. For example, THRIFTY (for THIRTY), FROSTY (for FORTY), AFFECTIONATELY (for FIFTY-ONE), and INTERCHANGEABILITY (for both EIGHTY-NINE and NINETY-EIGHT).

APRIL 20

Start both the timers together and pop the eggs into the boiling water. After seven minutes, when the smaller timer runs out, restart it. After eleven minutes, when the larger timer runs out, and the smaller timer has been running for four minutes since it was restarted, invert the smaller timer. It will then run for four more minutes, running out after 15 minutes. All told, then, I only have to spend 15 minutes to get 15-minute eggs.

APRIL 21

Because we cannot be weD without it. Because it comes at the end of beeF. Because it occurs at the end of LenT. The letters E–Z (=easy, phonetically).

APRIL 22

The fewest plus and minus signs is 4. This is the solution:
$$98 - 76 + 54 + 3 + 21 = 100$$

APRIL 23

William Shakespeare = We all make his praise. Saint George and the Dragon = Ha! A strong giant ended ogre.

APRIL 24

CHECKED stood out because it was the only word which could be read directly from the office stamp.

APRIL 25

Sparkling, sparking, sparing, spring, sprig, prig, pig, pi, I

APRIL 26

a. Bullitt b. Network c. Earthquake d. Annie Hall e. Jungle Book f. The Towering Inferno g. French Connection h. The Good, the Bad and the Ugly i. Butch Cassidy and the Sundance Kid j. Close Encounters of the Third Kind

APRIL 27

The goods trains come six minutes after the passenger trains. Thus, the boy's odds of arriving after a goods train and before a passenger train are 9 to 1, since for 54 out of every 60 minutes it is a passenger train that is expected.

APRIL 28

a. What's a Grecian urn? b. What's special about a brass band? c. What noise does a Japanese camera make? d. What have rainbow trout got that no other trout have? e. What do you get when you ask a woman her age? f. What's nu? g. What was the score in the carbon-uranium game? h. What was the slogan of that airline that went out of business?

APRIL 29

40 square yards

APRIL 30

Suppose there were x red cards in the first portion. Then there are 2x black cards in the first portion, (26 - x) red cards in the second portion, and (26 - 2x) black cards in the second portion. Hence $(26 - 2x)/(51 - 3x) = \frac{1}{3}$. From which x = 9. So there were originally 27 cards in the first portion, and 25 cards in the second portion.

MAY 1

Mayhem, mayonnaise, dismay, Romany, Monday, Maundy, embassy, mealy, amatory, imperially

MAY 2

Access, corset, crater, estate, seethe, street

MAY 3

The first number in alphabetical order is EIGHT. The last number is TWO THOUSAND TWO HUNDRED AND TWO.

MAY 4

The number of possible arrangements of the 26 letters is $26 \times 25 \times 24 \ldots \times 2 \times 1$. In each of the arrangements there are 23 positions in which the word IAGO can appear. For each position, the 22 remaining letters can be arranged in 22×21

$\times$ 20 ... $\times$ 2 $\times$ 1 ways. Therefore, the probability that IAGO appears is 23 $\times$ 22 $\times$ 21 ... $\times$ 2 $\times$ 1 divided by 26 $\times$ 25 $\times$ 24 ... $\times$ 2 $\times$ 1, which is equal to $\frac{1}{15600}$. Since the appearance of IAGO excludes the possibility that LEAR will also appear — the letter A being common — the probability that one or the other appears is the sum of their individual probabilities. Thus, 1 in 7800.

MAY 5

The pattern is illustrated by these examples from the puzzle: 31 = 3 $\times$ 9 + 4; 220 = 9 $\times$ 21 + 31; and 1081 = 21 $\times$ 41 + 220. So the missing number is equal to 220 $\times$ 1081 + 6949, or 244,769.

MAY 6

a. Vanity Fair (Thackeray) b. Sons and Lovers (Lawrence)
c. Nicholas Nickleby (Dickens) d. Huckleberry Finn (Twain)
e. Catcher in the Rye (Salinger) f. An Unsocial Socialist (Shaw) g. Animal Farm (Orwell) h. Ulysses (Joyce) i. Lolita (Nabokov) j. Dr. No (Fleming)

MAY 7

The words all have their letters occurring in alphabetical order. A similar five-letter word is BELOW, and ALMOST is a six-letter one.

MAY 8

The contents of the ten bags should be $1, $2, $4, $8, $16, $32, $64, $128, $256 and $489. Notice how the contents of the first nine bags are in geometrical progression.

MAY 9

Each of the answers read upside down spells out a word, name or phrase. Thus: a. 3704 (hole) b. 5710 (oils) c. 5733 (eels) d. 7105 (soil) e. 7714 (hill) f. 7734 (hell) g. 53751 (isles) h. 317537 (Leslie) i. 710.77345 (Shell oil) j. 3704.7734 (hell hole)

MAY 10

a. Protectionism b. violence c. anarchists d. infection e. militarism   f. legislation

MAY 11

The professor lived at number 204 in a street of 288 houses.

MAY 12

"Greatest idealist born" is the best we can manage.

MAY 13

The officer had 1975 men. When he formed a square measuring 44 by 44, he had 39 men over. When he tried to form a square 45 by 45, he was 50 men short.

MAY 14

The mixture contains $\frac{7}{24}$ wine and $\frac{17}{24}$ water.

MAY 15

It uses each letter of the alphabet at least three times.

MAY 16

If the cards are arranged in the 3-by-3 array below, this game emerges as a disguised version of noughts and crosses.

fish	soup	swan
girl	horn	army
knit	vote	chat

The eight columns, rows and diagonals may be characterized by the common letters: I, O and A for the columns, S, R and T for the rows, and H and N for the diagonals. Any noughts and crosses player knows that there is only one way to defend against a corner opening: by taking the center square. The only card which will prevent your opponent from winning is the one marked "horn." Once you take it, best play on both parts will result in a draw.

MAY 17

Averaging the times for a result of 1 minute is incorrect in both cases. In 1½ minutes the man can walk down 1 moving escalator or up 3. In 3 minutes' walking, half the time up and half the time down, he can walk four escalator lengths. This is his walking pace—four escalator lengths in 3 minutes—for the effect of the moving escalator is cancelled. He can, therefore, climb or descend the still escalator in ¼ of 3 minutes, that is, 45 seconds. In the 1½ minutes required to walk down the moving "up" escalator, he walks the equivalent of two still escalators. Therefore the escalator must have moved up once in that time and its speed is one length in 1½ minutes.

MAY 18

a. East, last, lest, west b. hate, have, hove, love c. heat, head, herd, here, hire, fire d. lead, load, goad, gold e. lion, loon, boon, boor, boar, bear f. dusk, tusk, Turk, lurk, lark, dark, darn, dawn

MAY 19

The man ordered 9 feet 2 inches of rope, and got 2 feet 9 inches.

MAY 20

a. OPEC b. ERA c. EPA d. NASA e. DDT

MAY 21

a. Greenwich b. Hartford c. Glasgow d. Calcutta e. Madrid f. Miami g. Newark h. Princeton i. Singapore j. Paris k. Chicago

MAY 22

They can ride three times as fast as they can walk, so three-quarters of their time must have been spent walking, and only a quarter in riding. Therefore, they rode for 2 hours, going 18 miles, and walked back in 6 hours.

MAY 23

a. nectar b. peanuts c. turnips d. cutlets e. haricot f. lobster g. sausage h. sardines i. maraschino j. Easter eggs l. lemons and melons

MAY 24

Mercury and Jupiter, both planets of the Solar System. (Both "raster" and "trinal" are in the Oxford English Dictionary.)

MAY 25

The woman had a 9-year-old daughter and 2-year-old twins. Since the census taker knew both the product and the sum of their ages, confusion could only arise if two or more sets of ages led to the same product and sum. Breaking 36 into three factors, only two sets of ages (9, 2, 2 and 6, 6, 1) lead to the same sum, 13. The woman's final piece of information told the census taker that there was only one oldest daughter, not two.

MAY 26

a. Mali (*not* Iceland) b. Peru c. Haiti d. Gabon e. Monaco f. Poland

MAY 27

Mark is $27\frac{1}{2}$ and Andrew is $16\frac{1}{2}$.

MAY 28

There are several 7-letter words: acceded, baggage, cabbage, defaced, and effaced. And at least one 8-letter word: cabbaged.

MAY 29

TYPEWRITER is usually considered as the longest word that can be typed using the letters QWERTYUIOP. There are several other 10-letter words, though: REPERTOIRE, PROPRIETOR and PERPETUITY. There are also a couple of 11-letter words, too: PROPRIETORY and RUPTUREWORT.

MAY 30

The longest common word is probably FLASKS. Larger dictionaries, though, show less common words such as HALAKAH, FLAGFALL, and HAGGADAH.

MAY 31

a. Rutgers, New Brunswick b. Yale, New Haven c. Tulane, New Orleans d. Duke, Durham e. Radcliff, Cambridge f. Vassar, Poughkeepsie

JUNE 1

Jungle, junket, journey, juvenile, journalese, Junoesque, jurisprudence, adjunctive, juncture, déjeuner

JUNE 2

TWO is 138, so that $138 \times 138 = 19044$. T must equal 1 and W must be less than or equal to 4, since THREE contains five digits. E must equal 4 as 44 is the only combination of two equal digits that can terminate a square. Hence, 0 is either 2 or 8. Trial and error then shows that TWO must be 138.

JUNE 3

Our best efforts are these: LETTERS (Little Etchings That Transcribe Every Readable Sound), ANAGRAM (Any New, Appropriate, Generally Rearranged, Alphabetic Message), ALPHABET (All Letters Pictured: Helps Any Bibliographic Effort Tremendously), PALINDROME (Particularly Adroit Language Image Nicely Duplicating Reversed Order Message Exactly), ACRONYM (A condensed Representation of Nomenclature Yielding Meaning).

JUNE 4

The lines quoted are from Longfellow's "Evangeline." The third of the lines is remarkable. Its 49 letters contain all 24 of the letters in the author's name, HENRY WADSWORTH LONGFELLOW. Did Longfellow deliberately weave his name into one of Evangeline's lines?

JUNE 5

Four seconds — two intervals of two seconds

JUNE 6

a. The Admirable Crichton (Barrie) b. Barchester Towers (Trollope) c. Cannery Row (Steinbeck) d. Dr. Jekyll and Mr. Hyde (Stevenson) e. Edwin Drood (Dickens) f. From Russia with Love (Fleming) g. Guy Mannering (Scott) h. Little Women (Alcott) i. No Highway (Shute) j. Utopia (More)

JUNE 7

The voting tied for Postman's Knock, with 156 for, 156 against, and 13 abstaining. For Strip Liar Dice, the voting was 169 for, 144 against, and 12 abstaining.

JUNE 8

At first glance, this seems impossible. After all, it appears that the only thing any of the applicants can know is that at least one black mark is visible, and clearly the problem cannot be solved with just that information. Therefore, something else must be known, but what? The really intelligent person realizes that he also knows something of the reasoning process that must be going on in the minds of the applicants, and the solution may lie in that fact. Since all three applicants raised their hands, the intelligent person reasons, there were two possibilities: two black and one white, or all three black. If, therefore, there were a white mark on any forehead, two men would see one black and one white and would instantly deduce that the third mark must be black. Since this instant solution did not occur, each of the three men saw two black marks. Therefore, all the marks were black, including that of the successful applicant.

JUNE 9

We managed to rearrange THE LIFE AND ADVENTURES OF NICHOLAS NICKLEBY in this phrase: FINE TALE: FIND THOU A NOVEL BY CHARLES DICKENS. Did you find anything better than that?

JUNE 10

Each of the 20 words is French, and when translated back into English, word by word, these ten combinations emerge: garlic bread, soiled oven, gold country, your thing, field goal, short hand, corner tooth, sand tower and bear cat.

JUNE 11

42 inches. Use of simple geometry reveals that the answer to this type of problem is always obtained by multiplying together the heights of the two poles, and then dividing this by the sum of the poles' heights. Thus, 78×91 divided by $78 + 91$.

JUNE 12

Entertainment, essentialness, underground, bleachable, outshout, bedaubed, Manxman

JUNE 13

Camel, Main, ago; megalomaniac

166

JUNE 14

Oh say [did] you realize this was the opening phrase of our National Anthem? The missing letters are S's and W's.

JUNE 15

Despite the number of missing prices, the solution can be found if you consider in turn the different numbers of lollipops and toffee sticks that might have been bought, looking for the common factor in the amounts of money left each time, which will be the price of the oranges. As the prices are realistic, a common factor of 1 is excluded. And the prices turn out to be 5 cents for an orange, 3 cents for a lollipop, and 4 cents for a toffee stick.

JUNE 16

Abuses, bustle, usurer, strove, eleven, serene

JUNE 17

Cried, blur, i.e.; irreducible

JUNE 18

Peter picks a peck in 48 minutes.

JUNE 19

David

JUNE 20

Ail, aim, bail, bilk, fed, fog, fop, for, form, gory, hilt, him, ilk, jab, jail, jilt, kilt, limn, milk, nog, prong, pronged, pyx, slim, slut

JUNE 21

A plump wench flagged a Zanzibar kayak to query a vivid chief squaw about juju maxixes.

JUNE 22

Ugly = offensive; offensive = insulting; insulting = insolent; insolent = proud; proud = lordly; lordly = stately; stately = grand; grand = gorgeous; gorgeous = beautiful. The transition

is in the equation of INSOLENT, a negative quality, with
PROUD, a positive quality.

JUNE 23

The categories are as follows: AMTUVWY (symmetrical about
the vertical axis; that is, the left and right halves are mirror
images of each other), BCDEK (symmetry about the horizontal axis; that is, the top and bottom halves are mirror images
of each other); FGJLNPQRSZ (no symmetry), and HIOX
(symmetry about both axis).

JUNE 24

The extra 6 yards will make the girdle and the earth almost
one yard apart for the entire length of the equator. The increase is independent of the original length of the girdle,
whether it is around the earth or a marble! Remember that
circumference = 2 × pi × radius. If the circumference increases by 6 yards, then the radius must increase by 6 yards
divided by 2 = pi. This works out to 34.2 inches, or just under
a yard.

JUNE 25

If a square number ends in identical digits, those digits must be
4, as in the case of 144, the square of 12. But there cannot be
more than three identical digits, and therefore the smallest
answer is 1444, the square of 38. (Note the relevance of this
solution to the puzzle for June 3.)

JUNE 26

a. Because one word leads to another b. Because there is a
host put out and not one guessed c. The letter A, because it
makes her hear d. Because it brings the proudest man to his
sneeze e. Because he is a pupil under the lash f. Time to
have the clock repaired g. An embarrassed zebra! (*Not* a newspaper, that's *read* all over) h. The letter M i. Courtship j.
Because he is pretty sure to be riddled to death

JUNE 27

The fare was 10 cents.

168

JUNE 28

a. fervent servant   b. prosaic mosaic   c. truculent succulent
d. granite planet   e. raucous caucus   f. dire choir

JUNE 29

a. came, cameo   b. Ides, ideas   c. crime, Crimea   d. lien, alien
e. rode, rodeo   f. whine, wahine

JUNE 30

a. Warren Beatty   b. Robert Redford   c. Al Pacino   d. Elliott
Gould   e. Barbra Streisand   f. Sean Connery   g. Walter Matthau   h. Glenda Jackson   i. Jane Fonda   j. Julie Andrews

JULY 1

Jubilantly, judicially, jugglery, justly, juvenility, adjunctly,
jejunely, joustily, injudiciously, conjugality

JULY 2

The five words in the five-by-five square are harps, aware, radar, prate, and seres.

JULY 3

Euclid's error amounted to multiplying by 49 instead of 409.
Divide the error by the difference (328,320 by 360), and you
will get the other number, 912.

JULY 4

Our best solutions are these:
  CREED DEFINED A CONTINENTAL HOPE
  PLAN ONCE DECIDED — FREE THE NATION!

JULY 5

Sufficient information is not available to justify a conclusion.

JULY 6

Call the teams D, A, B, M, and J (standing for Dew Drop Inn,
Atlantic Cafe, Blue Balloon, McSurley's and Jimmy's Tavern).
On the first Saturday, D played A. M must have played in the
other match, for they have their bye on the fourth Saturday.
But M plays B in the second round, so they play J in round

169

one, and B has the bye. J cannot have the bye in round two, for if they did, D would meet A, whom they have played already. And J cannot have the bye in round three, for they are playing B. So, on the fifth Saturday, J, Jimmy's Tavern, have the bye.

JULY 7

The party consisted of 2 little girls and a boy, their father and mother, and their father's father and mother.

JULY 8

317,537. The names result from entering the appropriate numbers on an electronic calculator and then reading them upside down.

JULY 9

Erases, regent, agenda, sender, endear, starry

JULY 10

Banana (123232), needed (122323), tattoo (121133), murmur (123123), redder (123321), effete (122131), deemed (122321), revere (123212), teethe (122132), cocoon (121-223), grotto (123443), coffee (123344)

JULY 11

The letter E

JULY 12

The river is 1760 yards (1 mile) wide. The times that the boats stayed at their slips is of no relevance.

JULY 13

The ages were 20 and 64.

JULY 14

Seven-letter words: BALLETS, BESTIAL, BILLETS, LIBATES. Six-letter words: ABLEST, BALLET, BILLET, STABLE. Five-letter words: BASTE, BEAST, BLAST, BLEAT, LABEL, LIBEL, SABLE, TABLE. Four-letter words: ABLE, BALE, BALL, BEAT, BELL, BELT, BEST, BIAS, BILE, BILL

JULY 15

Hat, lane, eight, gin; nightingale

JULY 16

The first time would be 5 and $\frac{5}{143}$ minutes past 12, which might also indicate $\frac{60}{143}$ minutes past 1. Or, expressed slightly less accurately, 5 minutes past 12 and about half a minute past 1.

JULY 17

John Stuart Mill was born in 1806. This would make him 43 years old in the square of his age (1849). People born in 1892 were 44 in the year 44 squared (that is, 1936). And people born in 1980 will be 45 in the year 45 squared (that is, 2025).

JULY 18

Four-score

JULY 19

Aunt, tusk, mils; gels, rate, spin; cart, mere, sump; inns, test, writ; buzz, earl, rope; rend, spin, tang; epee, join, shin; lamb, mart, over

JULY 20

I understand you undertake to undermine my undertaking.

JULY 21

This is one of many possible solutions:

17	24	1	8	15
23	5	7	14	16
4	6	13	20	22
10	12	19	21	3
11	18	25	2	9

All the rows, columns and diagonals add up to 65.

JULY 22

a. An inside job b. the heart of the matter c. see both sides of the question d. badinage e. undercover agent f. that is beside the point g. the first and last h. Constantinople

JULY 23

a. Sedate b. forbids c. Oliver Twist d. the morning after the night before e. short back and sides f. bedspread g. jack-in-a-box h. something in the air

JULY 24

Multiply 273863 by 365 and the product is 99959995. Working the problem backwards, any number whatever consisting of eight figures with the first four repeated is divisible by 73 (and by 137) without remainder, because 73 multiplied by 137 is 10001. If it ends with 5 or 0, it is divisible by 365, as 5 times 73 is 365. Knowing this, the highest possible product can be written down at once.

JULY 25

Caroline, the blonde hairdresser, is the oldest, Susan, the brunette receptionist, comes next. And Bernice, the red-headed typist, is the youngest.

JULY 26

"Chess is a foolish expedient for making idle people believe they are doing something very clever, when they are only wasting their time."

JULY 27

In 5 seconds, both trains (together) go 600 feet, or 120 feet per second. In 15 seconds, the faster train gains 600 feet, or 40 feet per second. Add together the sum and difference of the rates obtained, and divide by 2. This gives 80 feet per second as the speed of the faster train (roughly $54\frac{1}{2}$ miles per hour), from which it is clear that 40 feet per second is the speed of the slower train (roughly $27\frac{1}{3}$ miles per hour).

JULY 28

The nomads contributed 5, 4 and 3 pints. Sharing the 12 pints among four people gives each of them 3 pints. The third nomad therefore drank his entire contribution, and so should get paid nothing.

172

a. James Barrie b. Francis Drake c. Fidel Castro d. Daniel Defoe e. Adolf Hitler f. John Keats g. Henry Ford h. Karl Marx i. Martin Luther j. Jane Austen

5. Each value appears on an even number of squares, eight. Inside the chain, the values match in pairs. Therefore, a 5 at one end of the chain must be matched by a 5 at the other end.

a. Backward, wardrobe b. barren, render c. border, derive d. common, money e. curtain, tainted f. doorkey, keystone g. explain, plaintive h. fireside, sideways i. footstep, stepson j. fretsaw, sawmill

Resting, gaiters, retains, seating, strange, staring, erasing

Augustine, caught, inaugurate, daughter, laughable, accusing, catapulting, sausage, assuage, haughtiness

Withhold, skiing, bookkeeper, vacuum, navvy, powwow

a. China b. Yemen c. Crete d. Italy e. Nepal f. Niger g. Burma h. Sudan i. Angola j. Israel k. Cyprus l. Algeria

As it is evident that Camille, June and Martha received respectively $1220, $1320 and $1420, making together the $3960 left to the three wives, if Jack Smith receives as much as his wife Camille, $1220; Horace Saunders half as much again as his wife June, $1980; and Terry Connors twice as much as his wife Martha, $2840, then we have correctly paired the married couples and accounted for exactly $10,000.

$$3915 + 15 + 4826 = 8756$$

AUGUST 7

```
A P P L E
R E L A X
O R A T E
M I N E R
A L E R T
```

AUGUST 8

Your strategy should be quite different from that pursued in "Twenty Questions." One way to begin is to start with the question "Is your number bigger than 1?" If you get a YES response, your next question will be "Is your number bigger than 2?" and so on. In this manner, the first NO answer you receive will pinpoint your opponent's number, which you will promptly guess the next time you assume the role of questioner. The only way your opponent can win, therefore, is to guess your number on his first round of questions. His chance of doing this is 1 out of 100, so your advantage in this game, as first questioner, is 99 to 1. As the size of the range of numbers increases, the first player's advantage increases correspondingly.

AUGUST 9

D is for Handsome, E is for Twitched, F is for Neufchatel, G is for Gnome, H is for Myrrh, I is for Heifer, J is for Marijuana, K is for Knight, L is for Talk, M is for Mnemonic, N is for Autumn, O is for Leopard, P is for Psychologist, Q is for Cinq-cents, R is for Atelier, S is for Viscount, T is for Hautboy, U is for Plaque, W is for Writing, X is for Chateaux, and Y is for Pray. Don't worry if V defeats you—it did us!

AUGUST 10

If two widows had each a son, and each widow married the son of the other and had a daughter by the marriage, all the relationships will be found to result.

174

AUGUST 11

The only king who was crowned in England since the Conquest was James I, who was already king of Scotland. The question was not how many *men* have been crowned, but how many *kings* have been crowned!

AUGUST 12

Grouse, rouge, ogre, ego, go, o; grouse, rouse, rose, roe, or, o; grouse, roués, sour, sou, so, o

AUGUST 13

"Flit on, cheering angel" seems a particularly apt rearrangement of Florence Nightingale.

AUGUST 14

c. Viktor can outlift Boris by more than he can outlift Tam.

AUGUST 15

IVANHOE, BY SIR WALTER SCOTT can be anagrammed to give A NOVEL BY A SCOTTISH WRITER!

AUGUST 16

The second way is really the first way backwards! It, too, would take ⅔ of an hour to burn the candle out.

AUGUST 17

The letter V

AUGUST 18

a. The Wind in the Willows (Grahame) b. Winnie the Pooh (Milne) c. Women in Love (Lawrence) d. Wuthering Heights (Brontë) e. Westward Ho (Kingsley) f. Tom Jones (Fielding) g. Tono Bungay (Wells) h. The Snow Goose (Gallico) i. Rich Man, Poor Man (Shaw) j. Rikki Tikki Tavi (Kipling)

AUGUST 19

The mother and boy. Pitting the two winning teams against the two losing teams (boy + boy + girl + mother versus father + boy + girl + girl) will obviously result in a win for boy + boy

+ girl + mother over father + boy + girl + girl. Take a girl and a boy away from each side, and boy + mother must still beat father + girl.

AUGUST 20

Brian Brown drove the BMW, Alan Andrews drove the Avenger, and Colin Cooper drove the Cortina.

AUGUST 21

Culture vulture, dark horse, Welsh rabbit, Cheshire cat, black sheep, John Bull, queer fish, eager beaver, lame duck, desert rat. None is quite the same type of animal name as polar bear, and so on, which were mentioned in the puzzle!

AUGUST 22

The station clock is 3 minutes fast. The morning journey took 65 minutes, and the evening journey therefore took 52 minutes, and the train arrived 57 minutes after it should have left, that is, 3 minutes early.

AUGUST 23

a. origin, aborigines b. rust, frustrated c. sure, leisurely d. trim, matrimony e. spa, newspapers f. riot, patriots g. avenge, scavenger h. bell, rebellion i. ass, cassock j. ensure, censure

AUGUST 24

Here are two solutions:
$$17 + 82 + (\tfrac{45}{90}) + (\tfrac{3}{6}) = 100$$
$$49 + 50 + (\tfrac{38}{76}) + (\tfrac{1}{2}) = 100$$

AUGUST 25

$$7 + 1 = 8 \quad 9 - 6 = 3 \quad 4 \times 5 = 20$$

AUGUST 26

Ebbtide, accretion, oddment, offhand, egghead, withhold, jackknife, killjoy, immune, innkeeper, sapphire, myrrh, cesspool, cutthroat, navvy, glowworm

AUGUST 27

The hour indicated would be exactly 23 and one-thirteenth minutes after four o'clock. But because the minute hand moved in the opposite direction, the real time would be 36 and twelve-thirteenths minutes after four o'clock. You must deduct the number of minutes indicated from 60 to get the real time.

AUGUST 28

$$1 + 3 + 7 + (\tfrac{9}{5}) = 2 + 4 + 6 + .8$$

Both sides add up to 12.8.

AUGUST 29

a. Sweden   b. China   c. France   d. Wales   e. India   f. Canada

AUGUST 30

Surprisingly, the common letter N is the most likely stumbling block. There should be no trouble getting to N by means of armadillo, bear, cat, dog, elephant, fox, gorilla, horse, impala, jaguar, kangaroo, leopard, monkey. About the commonest land mammals whose names begin with N are NILGAI and NUTRIA, which are hardly likely to be known to the players. Whether NAG and NANNY GOAT would occur to anyone is doubtful. You'd have to be pretty sharp to think of either of those in 10 seconds.

AUGUST 31

The commonest letter in the English language, E, does not appear at all in the paragraph.

SEPTEMBER 1

```
T H E F T
H E L L O
R A D I O
O V E R T
B E R T H
```

SEPTEMBER 2

Steeplejack, thermometer, subterfuge; sepulchre, tempest, berkelium; transept, contempt, number; sleepy, stream, bleary

SEPTEMBER 3

a. Sopwith Camel b. one in a million c. Unfinished Symphony d. not before time e. Long Island f. Lover come back to me   g. six-shooters

SEPTEMBER 4

13.7 gallons at 46 cents = $6.30 (to the nearest $\frac{1}{2}$ ¢). Therefore my change from $20 was $6.30 as I had been charged $13.70.

SEPTEMBER 5

Oil, coil, colic; hat, chat, catch; ark, rack, crack; irk, rick, crick; tape, epact, accept; oust, scout, stucco; oast, coast, accost; rose, score, soccer; here, cheer, creche; near, crane, cancer; sear, scare, scarce; sour, scour, crocus; lean, lance, cancel; hate, teach, cachet; head, ached, cached; rile, relic, circle; lout, clout, occult; spite, septic, sceptic; nose, scone, sconce; neat, enact, accent

SEPTEMBER 6

Two hundred and six, two hundred and thirty

SEPTEMBER 7

157 squared is 24649, and 158 squared is 24964.

SEPTEMBER 8

Eleven and twelve

SEPTEMBER 9

Four.

SEPTEMBER 10

Peter Brady, artist, Dan Paine, salesman, and Jim Hall, chemist. The deputation of two was Peter Brady and Jim Hall.

SEPTEMBER 11

The car, when Richard met it, would have reached the station in another six minutes. So Richard had been walking for 30 minutes. Hence, had his wife met Richard at the station, he would have arrived 24 minutes earlier at the point where he actually met the car. So he would have arrived home at 5:36.

SEPTEMBER 12

CARE is a four-letter example, allowing SCARE, CHARE, CADRE, CARVE and CARES; CARES is a five-letter example, allowing SCARES, CHARES, CADRES, CARVES, CARETS, and CARESS.

SEPTEMBER 13

There are several ways in which this can be done. Here are just three: Orientals, latrines, nastier, satire, irate, tear, rat, at, a; Orientals, relation, elation, entail, alien, nail, nil, in, I; Orientals, entrails, salient, saline, leans, seal, sea, as, a.

SEPTEMBER 14

a. Abidable b. airmails c. bareback d. churches e. decadent f. epilepsy g. kamikaze h. lovelorn i. postpone j. tomatoes

SEPTEMBER 15

$$4973 \times 8 = 39784$$

SEPTEMBER 16

It is impossible to work out the cost per pound of each of the different nuts. However, the cost of various combinations can be worked out. If you combine $1\frac{1}{2}$ packets of the first kind ($3) with $\frac{1}{2}$ packet of the second kind ($1.50) and all of the third packet ($1.50), you get 3 pounds of each for $6. A mixture of 1 pound of each, therefore, should cost you $2.

SEPTEMBER 17

No, Annabelle is married to Benjamin Edwards, and he has the smallest annual income. Felix's wife is Iris Hayes.

SEPTEMBER 18

Opera, cough, and network

SEPTEMBER 19

Ambidextrous, favourite, behaviour, pneumonia, dialogue, disourage, consanguine, housemaid, ultraviolet, unsociable

SEPTEMBER 20

Water, whose chemical formula is H_2O (H to O); 3; none, as the longest rivers are the Nile and Amazon; incorrectly; N and T, these being the next letters composed solely of straight lines.

SEPTEMBER 21

The figure 8

SEPTEMBER 22

2.1 pounds. The "whole crab" must weigh 0.6 pounds, and the "half crab" 0.9 pounds, totalling 1½ pounds. If the former were halved and the latter doubled, the weights would then be 0.3 and 1.8 pounds, totaling 2.1 pounds.

SEPTEMBER 23

Each price was ⅝ of the previous price. So the next price will be $156.25.

SEPTEMBER 24

The diameter is 6.324 inches. If you place the point of a compass at the center of a black square on a chessboard with two inch squares, and extend the arms of the compass a distance equal to the square root of 10 inches (which is 3.162 inches), the pencil will trace the largest possible circle that touches only black squares. The diameter is, of course, equal to twice the radius.

SEPTEMBER 25

```
M A R S H
I R A T E
L E V E R
K N E A D
Y A N K S
```

SEPTEMBER 26

Thomas, moats, atom, mat, ta, a; Stearns, stares, tears, rate, eat, at, a; Eliot, tile, tie, it, I

SEPTEMBER 27

Defying, fighting, hijack, monopoly, querist, understudy

SEPTEMBER 28

76 and 109, the difference between successive numbers increasing by 6 each time; inches in a mile (63,360 to about

52,000); seconds in a week (604,800 to 528,000); square feet in half a square mile (about 14 million to 10½ million); one and four-elevenths

SEPTEMBER 29

```
M E R G E R S
E T E R N A L
R E G A T T A
G R A V I T Y
E N T I T L E
R A T T L E R
S L A Y E R S
```

SEPTEMBER 30

The shells were divided in the proportions 9:12:14. The youngest boy got 198, the next oldest got 264, and the oldest got 308. The boys' ages cannot be determined; all that we know is that they are in the proportion 9:12:14.

OCTOBER 1

Octillion, ocelot, concoction, occult, overact, rocket, conceited, oculist, concrete, occupant

OCTOBER 2

a. ionize b. day in, day out c. long time no see d. hole in one e. cleanliness is next to godliness f. the ends of the earth g. turn up your nose h. tin-tacks

OCTOBER 3

The number of goals scored by each team is the same as the number of vowels in the team's name as printed. So Philadelphia scored 5.

OCTOBER 4

They are all personal names spelled backwards.

OCTOBER 5

Round

OCTOBER 6

Never! Most of the information given is irrelevant. If the tails wind doubled its speed going, its velocity must have equaled that of the plane. On the way back, such a wind would effectively reduce the speed of the plane to zero.

OCTOBER 7
Stentorian, transient, entrains, nastier, astern, tears, sate, tea, at, a. This is just one of many possible solutions.

OCTOBER 8
Alison is the cashier; she lives with her sister and goes to work by bus. Brenda is the receptionist; she is married and walks to work. Carla is the secretary; she lives alone and drives to work.

OCTOBER 9
a. Straw Dogs b. Deliverance c. A Clockwork Orange d. Towering Inferno e. Midnight Cowboy f. Nashville g. Emanuelle h. The Godfather i. Last Tango in Paris j. Dirty Harry

OCTOBER 10
a. tendency b. tender c. tendon d. tendril e. tenement f. tenet g. tennis h. tensile i. tenor j. tense

OCTOBER 11
a. plane, ash, beech b. pine, elder, box c. pear, poplar, willow

OCTOBER 12
Put the pie in the oven and start both egg-timers. When the first one runs out, turn it over. (Elapsed time so far is 4 minutes.) When the second timer runs out, turn it over, too. When the first one runs out again (after a total of 8 minutes), the second timer has been running for one minute since it was restarted, so turn it over again. When the one minute runs out, the pie is ready.

OCTOBER 13
Charlie Baldwin, aged 24, drank most, followed in order by Allen Cox (aged 34), Brian Denby (aged 26), and David Ashton (aged 36).

OCTOBER 14

Apples and pears (stairs), bees and honey (money), butcher's hook (look), china plate (mate), daisy roots (boots), Dolly Varden (garden), pig's ear (beer), Rose Lee (tea), trouble and strife (wife), whistle and flute (suit)

OCTOBER 15

The shopkeeper supplied four boxes of 17 pounds and two boxes of 16 pounds, making up the 100 pounds as required.

OCTOBER 16

a. Life is far too important a thing ever to talk seriously about. b. It is absurd to divide people into good or bad. People are either charming or tedious. c. We are all in the gutter, but some of us are looking at the stars. d. One should always play fairly when one has the winning cards. e. Nothing spoils a romance so much as a sense of humour in the woman. f. If one tells the truth, one is sure, sooner or later, to be found out.

OCTOBER 17

a. fries, furies   b. purse, pursue   c. prise, uprise   d. gradate, graduate   e. em, emu   f. spine, supine   g. paper, pauper   h. fed, feud   i. do, duo   j. men, menu

OCTOBER 18

a. teepee   b. voodoo   c. assess   d. riffraff   e. giggling   f. referrer
Dreamt
g. eerie   h. llama   i. ooze
Value, which can be turned into valve

OCTOBER 19

The third and fourth powers must contain 10 digits between them, so the number sought can only be 18, 19, 20 or 21. Of these, 20 and 21 are bound to duplicate zeros and ones, respectively. Testing 18 and 19 reveals that 18 is the answer. The third and fourth powers of 18 are 5832 and 104,976.

OCTOBER 20

Ladder

OCTOBER 21

banana, parallax, charabanc, canasta, adamant, anagram, salaam, Malayan, catamaran, baccarat, abracadabra, macadam

OCTOBER 22

When the word YACHT is removed, the first and last letters of the remaining words spell out CHARLES DICKENS.

OCTOBER 23

a. Vic b. Ivan c. Sam d. Pat e. Abe f. Tom g. Hal h. Leo i. Sid j. Eric

OCTOBER 24

a. Liz b. Ada c. Eve d. Amy e. Marie f. Ella g. Sue h. Rita i. Anne j. Ruth

OCTOBER 25

Half dollar and nickel. One of the coins isn't a half dollar but the other *is*.

OCTOBER 26

The cost of the room was $27 minus $2, or $25. The error comes from mistakenly adding $27 and $2, and getting the misleading figure of $29.

OCTOBER 27

Mr. Jones is inexperienced.

OCTOBER 28

```
A S S E R T S
S L A V E R Y
S A L I V A S
E V I D E N T
R E V E R S E
T R A N S O M
S Y S T E M S
```

OCTOBER 29

RASH and RISK are two four-letter examples; TOPAZ and WEEPS are five-letter examples; and WETTISH is a seven-letter example. Did you find any words longer than seven letters?

OCTOBER 30

The latter (about 3.6 million to 10 million); seconds in a month (about 1.6 million to 2.6 million); 3; $22 + 2 = 24$; $33 - 3 = 30$ and $5 \times 5 + 5 = 30$ and $6 \times 6 - 6 = 30$

OCTOBER 31

Have you any eggs? Yes, we have eggs. Have you any ham? Yes, we have ham. Okay, I'll have ham and eggs.

NOVEMBER 1

Novelty, innovation, controversy, unconvinced, unmoved, unobvious, renovate, introvert, supernova, involved

NOVEMBER 2

The initial letters of the eight lines spell out PUZZLING. Additionally, and somewhat harder to spot, is that the 8th letter in the first line, the 9th letter in the second line, the 10th letter in the third line, and so on, spell out SOLUTION. We did ask you if you could find the solution!

NOVEMBER 3

Pneumonic gnomes knew mnemonic names. Ptomaine poisons Pnom-Penh's psychedelic philosophers.

NOVEMBER 4

The two ways of selling are only identical when the number of apples sold at 30 for $1 and 20 for $1 is in the proportion of 30 to 20.

NOVEMBER 5

If N is the total number of rockets, we can see that one tenth of N is equal to one-half of N minus one-sixth of N minus 21. So, N, which is also George's age, equals 90. He will be 100 in ten years' time.

185

NOVEMBER 6

The faster watch gains on the slower one at the rate of three minutes every hour. After 20 hours, the faster one will be ahead by one hour.

NOVEMBER 7

Precariousness, repercussions, preciousness, percussions, supersonic, conspires, princess, pincers, prince, price, pier, rip, pi, I

NOVEMBER 8

Eight marks are required. They are to be placed at the 1, 3, 6, 13, 20, 27, 31 and 35 inch positions.

NOVEMBER 9

This is just one of many possible arrangements:

```
 1 35 34  3 32  6
30  8 28 27 11  7
24 23 15 16 14 19
13 17 21 22 20 18
12 26  9 10 29 25
31  2  4 33  5 36
```

NOVEMBER 10

Emeer, reference, reverence, reservedness, peeresses, emergence, evergreen, sentencer, excrescence, elevenses, beppepered, telemetered

NOVEMBER 11

The decimal number 3.750 fills the bill, as well as a considerable number of improper fractions, including $\frac{10}{5}$, $\frac{24}{6}$, $\frac{54}{9}$, $\frac{36}{12}$, and $\frac{63}{21}$.

NOVEMBER 12

As the zoo contained two freaks, the four-footed bird and the six-legged calf, there must have been 24 birds and 12 beasts in all.

NOVEMBER 13

a. Iran b. Spain c. Persia d. Romania e. Bermuda f. Surinam g. Botswana h. Greenland i. Palestine j. Singapore k. San Marino l. Argentine

NOVEMBER 13

a. Franklin D. Roosevelt b. Cole Porter c. Jane Fonda d. Henry Ford e. Bette Davis f. Dolly Parton g. Ronald Reagan h. Andy Warhol i. Abe Lincoln j. Julia Child

NOVEMBER 15

a. lace b. crepe c. linen d. denim e. voile f. satin g. calico h. sateen i. worsted j. chenille k. dungaree l. gabardine

NOVEMBER 16

There is not just one other starting-point; there is an infinite number. Imagine a circle drawn around the *South* Pole at a distance of about 1.16 miles from the Pole. Start from any point on the circle. After walking a mile south, your next walk of one mile east will take you on a complete circle around the Pole, and the walk one mile north from there will return you to the starting-point. So, the starting-point could be of an infinite number of points on this circle of radius 1.16 miles centered on the South Pole. But that's not all. You could also start at points closer to the Pole, so that the walk east would carry you twice around the South Pole, or three times, or four times, and so on.

NOVEMBER 17

a. Casablanca (1942) b. Footlight Parade (1933) c. For Whom the Bell Tolls (1943) d. Stagecoach (1939) e. The Grapes of Wrath (1940) f. Here Comes Mr. Jordan (1941) g. Key Largo (1948) h. Little Caesar (1930) i. Things to Come (1936) j. Flying Down to Rio (1933)

NOVEMBER 18

Either man should be asked the following question: "If I were to ask you if this is the way I should go, would you say yes?" While asking the question, the hiker should be pointing at either of the directions going from the fork.

NOVEMBER 19

a. Hopalong Casserole b. nose job c. Tarzan Stripes Forever

a. Oder   b. Avon   c. Forth   d. Rhone   e. Hudson   f. Red Nile
g. Nile   h. Marne   i. Loire   j. Irtysh   k. Dniester   l. Savannah

a. one over the eight   b. contests   c. pins and needles   d. dunderhead   e. prime mover   f. Stonehenge   g. Monaco

Reasoning this out by starting from the end, we find that (1) the Anti-Tobacco League must obviously be opposed to the cigarette companies, (2) pamphlets attacking the League displease the League and please the manufacturers, (3) distributors of these pamphlets displease the League and please the manufacturers, (4) pickets opposing the distribution please the League and displease the manufacturers, (5) police interfering with the pickets displease the League and please the manufacturers, (6) injunction restraining the police pleases the League and displeases the manufacturers, and (7) vacating this injunction displeases the League and pleases the manufacturers. So, the answers to the original questions must be: (a) yes, at no longer being restrained (but if you answered that they didn't care one way or the other that would be acceptable), (b) no, the pickets were not pleased, (c) yes, the distributors were pleased, (d) yes, the cigarette companies were pleased, and (e) no, the League was not pleased.

No pawnbrokers are dishonest.

$$0 = 4 + 4 - 4 - 4 \qquad 1 = 44/44$$
$$2 = (4/4) + (4/4) \qquad 3 = (4 + 4 + 4)/4$$
$$4 = 4 + [4 \times (4 - 4)]$$
$$5 = \frac{(4 \times 4) + 4}{4}$$
$$6 = \frac{4 + 4}{4} + 4$$
$$7 = (44/4) - 4$$
$$8 = 4 + 4 + 4 - 4$$
$$9 = 4 + 4 + (4/4)$$
$$10 = (44 - 4)/4$$

NOVEMBER 25

The sick lad becomes an adult, he marries a girl from Australia, and she reads to him, just as his mother did, when he is ill. You should now be in a position to imagine him plaintively inquiring, 'What did you bring the book that I do not wish to be read on to out of up from Down Under for?' Nine prepositions! Did you do better than that?

NOVEMBER 26

666 yards; one-fourteenth of a week; 666 millimeters; 666 days; 666 inches; 28 days

NOVEMBER 27

(1) The one you did *after* the one you did *before* this one IS *this one*. In other words: (2) ". . . . the puzzle you solved *after* you solved the puzzle you solved *before* you solved this one" IS *this one* (3) Hence the question may be rephrased this way: "If the puzzle you solved *before* this one was harder than THIS ONE, was the puzzle you solved before this one harder than THIS ONE?" (4) The answer to this question is obviously YES.

NOVEMBER 28

Bankruptcy, blacksmith, pathfinder, formidable, discourage, championed, phlegmatic, lynching, outlandish, piccolo

NOVEMBER 29

The printer must have purchased the following 27 types:
AABCDEEEFGHIJLMNOOPRRSTUUVY

NOVEMBER 30

Wander, warden; drawn, wader, waned; awed, dawn, draw, wade, wand, wane, ward, warn, wend, wren; awe, awn, daw, dew, new, raw, wad, wan, war, wed

DECEMBER 1

Decade, decorate, drench, sidecar, bedecked, condescend, predilection, despotic, deduce, bandersnatch

DECEMBER 2

Each of the sentences is a palindrome. That is, the same letters occur backwards as well as forwards.

189

DECEMBER 3

a. Naturalist b. associated c. scrupulous d. fascinated e. precaution f. orchestral g. commentary h. infidelity i. ingredient j. woodpecker k. revolution l. telephones

DECEMBER 4

Dan Duryea, Ray Charles, Mel Torme, Burt Lancaster, Rock Hudson, Dean Martin, Lena Horne, Merle Oberon, Lorne Green, Cesar Romero, Barbra Streisand, Ernest Borgnine

DECEMBER 5

To reconstruct the number, it is only necessary to try different digits at the start of the sequence X10112 and divide by X to see whether the answer starts 10112. The only digit for which this works is 9. So, starting the division:

$$910112 / 9 = 101123 \text{ (remainder 5)}$$

Transferring the 3 also to the left-hand number:

$$9101123 / 9 = 1011235 \text{ (remainder 8)}$$

Transferring the 5, and so on, we finally reach a digit 9 with a zero remainder. This is the answer:

10112359550561797752808988764044943820224719

As was pointed out in the puzzle, the calculator did have an exceptionally long display!

DECEMBER 6

a. Diffident b. dissident c. millimeter d. unarranged e. inessential f. sniffing g. grammar h. quarreller i. mademoiselles j. assesses k. risottos l. staccato

DECEMBER 7

a. Grip, mesh, oven b. cone, Ural, this c. meal, dice, ohms d. come, pure, tits e. surd, pear, bode f. earl, tiny, sung g. ions, mint, sets h. amps, hone, cote i. whet, ears, tars j. atom, urge, reed

DECEMBER 8

It is a rewrite of the well-known nursery rhyme "Mary Had a Little Lamb" such that the letter E does not occur anywhere.

DECEMBER 9

USHERS contains US, SHE, HE, HER and HERS. SMITHERY yields HE, HER, HERS, HIM, HIS, I, IT, ITS, ME, MY, SHE, THEIR, THEIRS, THEM, THEY, THY and YE.

DECEMBER 10

❧ If you multiply 6,666 by the sum of the four given digits, you will get the correct answer. As 1, 2, 3 and 4 sum to 10, the required answer is 66,660.

DECEMBER 11

21. The first die is marked 16, 17, 18, 19, 20 and 21. The second die is marked —15, —9, —3, 3, 9 and 15.

DECEMBER 12

1 ton; 250 centimeters; 3 raised to the 5th power; zero degrees Centigrade; inches in a kilometer; -40 degrees Centigrade and -40 degrees Fahrenheit are equally cold.

DECEMBER 13

a. brag, garb b. revel, lever c. paws, swap d. laud, dual e. mood, doom f. warts, straw g. step, pets h. debut, tubed i. snip, pins j. evil, live

DECEMBER 14

Dwight Boone had the cheese sandwich, and Ed Arkwright had milk, a ham sandwich, and pie.

DECEMBER 15

a, rip, enripen b. crib, escribes c. eland, Icelandic d. row, ingrowing e. cent, recenter f. ale, stalest g. able, stablest h. men, tormentor

DECEMBER 16

Shackleton is the copilot, Campbell is the navigator, Garfield is the pilot, and Colson is the engineer.

DECEMBER 17

This one depends on your imagination!

DECEMBER 18

a. Maverick b. Cheyenne c. Butch Cassidy d. Hopalong Cassidy e. Bronco f. The Lone Ranger g. Rowdy Yates h. Ben Cartwright i. Joshua Smith j. Wyatt Earp

DECEMBER 19

TEAMMATE is an English word whose Russian cipher equivalent also happens to be the word TEAMMATE! The English word SNEER becomes CHEEP when "translated" into Russian in the prescribed manner.

DECEMBER 20

The letter C. Reading in a clockwise spiral from the top right-hand corner reveals the word:

PHANTASMAGORICAL

DECEMBER 21

a. Andorra b. Finland c. Congo d. Libya (Li by a) e. New Guinea f. Long Island g. Minorca h. Montana (M on T, an A) i. Vermont j. Rwanda

DECEMBER 22

Each letter of HALLS can be changed so as to make a new word: calls, hills, hails, halts, hallo. And SHORES is a six-letter example: chores, stores, shares, shoves, shorts, shored.

DECEMBER 23

A book of 10 letters could only be Colossians or Revelation. A chapter of 6 letters could be eleven, twelve or twenty. This eliminates Colossians because it has only four chapters. (Neither book has thirty chapters.) A verse of 7 letters could be fifteen or sixteen. The three chapters above (the 11th, 12th and 20th in Revelation) all have at least 15 verses, so any of the three are eligible. Chapters 11 and 12 in Revelation have *more* than one five-letter word in both verses 15 and 16. In Chapter 20, however, verse 15 contains only one 5-letter word which, oddly enough, is FOUND!

DECEMBER 24

a. tinsel b. reindeer c. brandy d. stockings e. seasons f. winter g. mince pies h. candles i. seasonal greetings

DECEMBER 25

(1) Christmas, Chartism, charism, charms, march, harm, ham, am, a (2) St. Nicholas made trim (3) It charms mites (4) loan, mule, sexy; only, axle, muse; ayes, mull, oxen

DECEMBER 26

a. Chit, rash, smit b. sent, soar, ales c. wine, trot, Tass d. deer, syce, comb e. yarn, this, seed (and also this, year, send) f. rein, deed, rise g. then, last, moth h. wits, best, week i. perk, suns, tier j. oral, vent, rely

DECEMBER 27

a. Hamlet, lettuce b. Handsome, somebody c. housework, workman (or houseboat, boatman) d. mischief, chieftain e. present, sentence f. prowess, essence g. pursuit, suitable (or purport, portable) g. sunset, settee i. tasty, tyrant j. warfare, farewell

DECEMBER 28

a. The Maltese Falcon (1941) b. National Velvet (1944) c. The Mask of Fu Manchu (1932) d. Gold Diggers of 1933 (1933) e. The Roaring Twenties (1939) f. Citizen Kane (1941) g. Mutiny on the Bounty (1935) h. Top Hat (1935) i. Footlight Parade (1933) j. The Big Sleep (1946) k. A Night at the Opera (1935)

DECEMBER 29

Wit so great will lead man; a man to wield great wills; go, administrate law well; at will, great wise old man

DECEMBER 30

Out of at least 48 items in the book, at least 6 were algebra problems and at least 4 were logic puzzles.

DECEMBER 31

Mahogany